"As a fan of both gratitude and year-long projects, I was hooked from the start. This book inspired me to write notes to everyone from coworkers to college friends, which helped me defy the gloomy apocalyptic mind-set that has overtaken so many of us."

—A. J. JACOBS, AUTHOR OF *THANKS A THOUSAND*

"Gina Hamadey has a way with words, with friends, with neighbors, with those tugging feelings we all have that maybe we've forgotten what's important. *I Want to Thank You* is a tonic for our times. It will cheer your day, guide you back to what matters most, and remind you of the power you have to make someone else feel special—most especially the ones you love. Thank you for this lovely book."

—BRUCE FEILER,
AUTHOR OF THE *NEW YORK TIMES*–BESTSELLING *LIFE IS IN THE TRANSITIONS* AND *THE SECRETS OF HAPPY FAMILIES*

"Gina makes me want to slow down, to reconnect, and, most of all, to appreciate the life I have, in all of its challenges and complexities. Thank you, Gina, thank you."

—EMMA STRAUB,
AUTHOR OF *ALL ADULTS HERE* AND OWNER OF BOOKS ARE MAGIC

"Gina Hamadey is a great storyteller. I love her references to finding ways to notice the little things and put down your phone—subjects near and dear to me."

—BARBARA ANN KIPFER,
AUTHOR OF *14,000 THINGS TO BE HAPPY ABOUT*

I WANT TO
THANK
YOU ♥

I WANT TO THANK YOU

How *a* Year of Gratitude
Can Bring Joy *and* Meaning *in*
a Disconnected World

 GINA HAMADEY

A TARCHERPERIGEE BOOK

tarcherperigee

an imprint of Penguin Random House LLC
penguinrandomhouse.com

Most TarcherPerigee books are available at special quantity discounts for bulk purchase for
sales promotions, premiums, fund-raising, and educational needs. Special books or book
excerpts also can be created to fit specific needs. For details, write:
SpecialMarkets@penguinrandomhouse.com.

Library of Congress Cataloging-in-Publication Data
Names: Hamadey, Gina, author.
Title: I want to thank you: how a year of gratitude can bring joy and
meaning in a disconnected world / Gina Hamadey.
Description: New York: TarcherPerigee, 2021.
Identifiers: LCCN 2020023354 (print) | LCCN 2020023355 (ebook) | ISBN
9780593189627 (hardcover) | ISBN 9780593189634 (ebook)
Subjects: LCSH: Gratitude.
Classification: LCC BF575.G68 B47 2021 (print) | LCC BF575.G68 (ebook) |
DDC 179/.9—dc23
LC record available at https://lccn.loc.gov/2020023354
LC ebook record available at https://lccn.loc.gov/2020023355

Printed in China

1   3   5   7   9   10   8   6   4   2

Book design by Lorie Pagnozzi

For Jake, Henry, and Charlie

CONTENTS

I WANT TO

THANK

YOU ♥

INTRODUCTION

I n the early spring of 2020, as a global pandemic shut down life as we knew it, I started noticing another infectious outbreak. All around me, people faced extreme isolation or claustrophobic togetherness; relentless tedium or crippling uncertainty; fear of losing their jobs, their homes, their loved ones—and yet they responded with an outpouring of gratitude.

My friend who was living apart from her ER doctor husband was "overcome with joy and gratitude" for those who "brought my husband dinner every night, put signs on our lawn and did nightly walk-bys to keep him company when he was alone." A college friend working at a hard-hit New Jersey hospital was "thankful for every person who stays home, physically distances, and wears a mask, despite these things being boring, lonely, frustrating, uncomfortable, sweaty, itchy, a little gross, and generally awkward."

A teacher shared that she was grateful, simply, for the past. "The uncertainty of the future," she said, "makes me appreciate even more the experiences and memories I've accumulated throughout my life."

Others reported being grateful for the chance to sit down to family dinner every night, to renew connections with friends, "to put down the phone and pick up a badminton racket," to savor things they normally overlooked. "I love what catches my son's eyes," said a former colleague who had begun taking daily walks with her young child. "Today he discovered a cool tree that I have bicycled by many times without noticing the unique roots that are exposed above the ground."

I heard a lot of appreciation for nature. My sister felt a kinship with the trees outside her Brooklyn apartment, a neighbor treasured "the spring blooms and the birds chirping and the evening golden hour," and a mentor delighted even in the pesky squirrels nibbling at her vegetable seedlings.

My mom, who was sheltering alone, said that "although so far away from my children, grandchildren, and family, my gratitude and peace lies in the fact that you are all well and safe."

In the absence of a cure or a vaccine, I was reminded of one of the grandest lessons I learned from the year I spent writing 365 thank you notes: Gratitude is strong medicine. It helps us see what's there instead of pining for what's missing. It spurs empathy and compassion and is an antidote to self-centered whining. (Although a little whining—ideally on the phone with an old friend, mezcal in hand— can be necessary and therapeutic.)

As friends and family members were sharing their gratitude, I was finishing up this book, and certain passages took on new meaning. I no longer had to persuade people that it was important to maintain connections despite the distance between us. Pleasures I had taken for granted—traveling, going to restaurants, throwing dinner parties—became impossible dreams. And thanking health-care workers, as I did for an entire month, became standard practice.

At our home in Brooklyn, the most heartening part of the day came at 7:00 p.m., when my neighbors stuck their heads out of windows and stepped onto balconies to clap and cheer and bang on pots to show their appreciation for the essential workers. "Go, doctors!" my two boys yelled. "You can do it—I know you can!" It was a daily reminder of what I spent my Thank You Year learning—that gratitude is what we have to give. It is free, and yet it has worth. Saying thank you became more than a nice thing to do. It became essential.

And it remained essential even as widespread injustice boiled over into raging protests. In New York City, the seven o'clock clapping continued even when there was an eight o'clock curfew. Gratitude and anger were not incompatible. We could applaud the brave people in our community *and* protest the world's evils.

It's difficult to imagine in this moment, but I know we will once again meet in restaurants, walk down crowded sidewalks, go to Broadway shows, and make small talk with neighbors while looking at their unobstructed faces. Maybe as you read this we are already there. Perhaps there's part of you that misses the glow of gratitude that was a bright spot in an otherwise dark and scary time.

This book is a blueprint for incorporating gratitude into your life in a lasting way. The good news is that you don't have to write 365 thank you notes, as I did. You get to decide how many notes you like to write in your Thank You Year: It could be one card every week or one per month. Or you can save on postage and call an old friend or email a long-ago mentor. If you do any of the above, you'll start to experience the many benefits of expressing gratitude. I hope it brings as much joy and connection to your life as it has to mine.

CHAPTER ONE

JANUARY: CHARITY

How Writing Thirty-One Notes to Generous Hearts Launched a Thank You Year

BENEFIT: Expressing gratitude feels good.

SURPRISE: I like writing thank you notes?

LESSON: Planning a Thank You Year illuminates what's important.

Monday morning in a New Jersey Transit train car was the inverse of my weekend: hushed instead of hectic, soothing instead of overstretched. Blessed solitude. I settled into a seat, looked at the bare trees whipping past the window, and pulled out my phone.

"Next stop, Summit!" the conductor said. *What happened to the last fifty minutes?* I wondered vaguely as I packed my bag, disembarked, and walked from the suburban New Jersey train station to the office of the home goods startup Boll & Branch, where I'd recently started a consulting gig.

After spending the day writing marketing copy about soft sheets and high-functioning pillows, I started the commute back to Brooklyn, boarding the train to repeat the blissful ride that again went by far too fast.

Expressing Gratitude Feels Good

When I settled into a train seat the next day, I kept my phone in my bag and instead pulled out a stack of thank you cards embossed with green palm trees. I'd put off this task long enough. "Dear Aunt Dot," I wrote. "Thank you for contributing so generously to our City Harvest drive. After much deliberation, Henry has decided that your food is . . . broccoli!"

My then-four-year-old's party trick was to assign everyone a food or drink that suited them: I was a tomato; my husband, Jake, was seltzer; our one-year-old Charlie was a sweet potato. I'd promised Henry-enhanced thank you notes as an incentive to City Harvest fundraiser donors the previous month, in December, and we raised more than $4,000. Now I needed to write those cards.

That morning Henry and I had a conversation about the first batch of contributors, and Henry declared that Aunt Dot was broccoli (a compliment, as it was his favorite vegetable), and other note recipients embodied a meatball, a banana peel, a carrot, and "a can of strawberries."

As the train entered Summit station, I stuffed seven completed cards into their box, tucked it into my backpack, and walked to the office. It was a crisp snowy day: The sky was a saturated blue, the snow a sparkly white. I walked by a glimmering steel diner and pun-happy mom-and-pop shops—Faux Paws Wholesome Pet Shop, a chocolate store called Sweet Nothings, McCools Ice Cream. I ordered a latte at the cozy Boxwood Coffee shop, humming the *Gilmore Girls* theme song. *That's* what this town reminded me of, I realized: the show's idyllic Stars Hollow. I'd been working here for two weeks, and I'd only just thought of it.

Over the next week's commutes, I alternated between writing the remaining thank you notes and scrolling through my social feeds. I

started to notice something: On the days when I would write, the ride seemed to slow, and I would leave the train feeling as though a veil had been lifted. I felt hopeful, optimistic, and *present*—a mood that would carry into my day. On the days when I would lose myself in social feeds, I would emerge feeling distracted, restless, almost ragged.

Wait a second. Did I *like* writing thank you notes?

I Like Writing Thank You Notes?

We can agree that thank you notes are kind of the worst, right? Obligations in three-by-five packages. There's the association, for starters: Someone—likely your mother—would pester you to just *write those thank you notes. You have a stack of birthday presents; the* least *you can do is express your gratitude.* And she was right, of course. It *is* the right thing to do—it's common courtesy. But it's presented as a chore, and so it feels like one. It's the very essence of etiquette, but even the word "etiquette" feels stuffy and goody-two-shoes. Who are we, Southern belles with crossed ankles?

And so, throughout my life, when faced with a stack of thank you cards, I would let out a Pavlovian yawn. That's why I stalled on thanking guests for their generous wedding presents for six months or more. I had a year to complete them, right? Or was it wedding guests who had a full year to send a gift? (Again, etiquette is not my area of expertise.)

Now, whenever I visit new parents, bearing lentil soup and some adorably tiny sweater, I implore them to please forget the thank you card. I refuse to add to their long, breast-milk-stained to-do list. (Let me take this opportunity to say: That directive still stands, despite my recent thank you note conversion.)

Standard thank you cards are boring—to write and to receive. What is there to say? It's a confirmation of receipt: *I got the thing you gave me, and I really liked it.* The most colorful copy you can hope to add is how you plan to use the object. *I plan to bring this beautiful navy sweater on my trip to Denver.*

What made these notes different?

For one thing, the recipients had not handed me a present. They had given money to City Harvest—an organization that rescues food that would have gone to waste and redirects it to hungry New Yorkers—just because I asked if maybe they could. And perhaps because they were mildly curious about the food that matched their personality, according to one sweet four-year-old.

I scanned the long list of people who contributed to my drive. It was an entirely random sampling of people in my life: an old writing coach, our real estate agent, college pals who had moved to London, my estranged friend Sara's ex-boyfriend. Every time I checked my online fundraiser page and spotted a new name, I felt a jolt of delight. It was nice to relive that feeling for a few moments as I thanked those generous hearts with a pen and my full attention, rather than tossing off a form email or a text.

And, obligation or etiquette aside, seeing my sincere words written in my off-kilter, half-messy mix of print and cursive on a piece of card stock lent my sentiment weight. I touched the card with my hands, and the recipient would, too. It was tactile, solid. The only way I interacted with most of those people was through social media; compared to that ersatz connection, this felt real.

I completed my final note—my friend Jennifer reminded Henry of "rainbow ice cream"—and watched dozens of cards vibrate on the train's tray table. Oddly, I felt sad that the task was completed. I wanted more of that pleasant, focused feeling I got from writing . . . how many cards? I glanced at my checked-off list of recipients: thirty-one.

Huh, I thought. *That's funny. I've written thirty-one cards, and it's January 31. I've written a thank you note for every day this year.*

What if I keep it up?

A thank you note for every day of the year. It had a nice ring to it. I used to make elaborate New Year's resolution lists ("learn to make tortillas from scratch," "make time for phone calls with California friends"). But that was in my twenties, before I had kids. In my childbearing thirties, the New Year functioned mostly as a reminder to lose whatever baby weight I felt I was carrying. I missed having a tangible, achievable goal that had nothing to do with my body or my career.

It was ambitious. There were 365 reasons why it was impractical to take on a time-consuming project when I was busy with my job and two little kids, not to mention a marriage and parents and siblings and friends—most of whom I hadn't seen in months or more. But maybe a project like this would help us reconnect?

Perhaps I would find the time by putting down my phone more often—another added benefit.

Of course, I could simply make an effort to incorporate thank you note writing into my life, with no specific target number to hit. But I knew, even as this flimsy thought materialized, that the half-goal wouldn't go anywhere. I was thirty-eight years old, squarely in life's rush hour, where good intentions sputtered and died. If I wanted to make thank you notes part of my life, I would need a specific goal and a solid action plan.

Would I stick to it, though? What was my motivation, beyond the sense that writing these notes would continue to feel good and that they would keep me off my feeds? Was that motivation strong enough to see me through the year?

I opened my gray notepad and wrote at the top:

REASONS TO WRITE 365 THANK YOU NOTES THIS YEAR

- ♥ Reconnect to parts of my life that I miss.
- ♥ Put out something positive in a time of despair.
- ♥ Return to something I love—writing with pens and paper.
- ♥ Get back in touch with people who mean something to me.
- ♥ See what good things come of it.

Reconnect to parts of my life that I miss. I'd been feeling . . . not unhappy. This is not a redemption story about a miserable woman who earns her happy ending. I was already content, lucky: I knew I had much to be grateful for—my health, my family, my work.

But. It felt like time was speeding up, whipping by faster than the

New Jersey towns out the window, and I needed to find a way to slow it down. My hours were spent hustling—after my two small kids, after freelance gigs, after a moment to myself. I would often think of a friend I hadn't spoken to in months, or a book I meant to read, but before I could reach out to the friend or jot down the title, the thought would be replaced by something more urgent. It was as if pieces of my life that were once beloved to me were floating around the room like confetti, ephemeral, just out of reach.

My mind felt as scattered as that confetti. I lived in triage—every moment tending to the neediest child, or client, or bill. Would retrieving memories from years when I had more time for relationships and hobbies and pleasure help me reconnect to those things?

It seemed like my friends were accepting their new roles more easily. I was having trouble embracing mine (Brooklyn mom, freelance cookbook writer, content marketer) and letting go of my numerous former identities (California girl, magazine editor, food and travel writer, capable dinner party host, friend connector, insatiable reader). Were those old versions of myself still inside me, still accessible?

Put out something positive in a time of despair. A month before the New Jersey train rides, I'd walked around our Brooklyn neighborhood scoffing at the beautifully adorned Christmas trees displayed in brownstone windows, which had seemed like nothing more than artifice. *The world is terrifying and depressing,* I thought. *Why staple shiny blinking lights on it?* I'd transmogrified into Scrooge, despite having loved Christmas all my life. When I was a kid, I would sit beneath our tree every night before bed, singing "Silent Night" to myself.

I used to be a relentlessly positive person. Maybe putting positivity into the world would improve my own outlook.

And yes, the news seemed to signal the end of days, with reports of creeping corruption and greed. But if it *was* the end of days, did I want to spend it burrowing in my phone, scared and alone? Or did I want to spend it forging and strengthening connections and expressing gratitude for the world's many kindnesses?

The bright spot of the holiday season, the part that hadn't felt like an act, was raising all that money for City Harvest. Working with the nonprofit and writing those cards had gotten me out of my head, with its running (sprinting!) to-do list. I wanted to extend that vacation from my own mind.

Return to something I love—writing with pens and paper. I write for a living, about soft sheets, new Caribbean hotels, nacho recipes, 25 Easy Thanksgiving Hacks! My personal writing—journals, an abandoned rom-com novel, children's books about Stubby the Toe and the Chew Chew Train that I'd only shown my kids—lay dormant. I hoped that writing for myself would be creatively fulfilling. And my handwriting might improve in the process, who knows.

Get back in touch with people who mean something to me. Of course, I wasn't going to be writing just for myself. Each note would have an audience of one—and I was hoping that, one by one, I would reconnect with people who once meant a lot to me, and who now, by virtue of their not living within walking distance, I hadn't seen in years.

In short, I had been feeling distracted, disengaged, and disconnected, and I wanted to become more focused, engaged, and connected.

Planning a Thank You Year Illuminates What's Important

Once I convinced myself that my motivations were strong enough to sustain the project, I got excited. This would be my—drum roll, please—Thank You Year.

I avoided the word "gratitude" because it had always struck me as hopelessly earnest. "Gratitude" rhymes with "platitude." Gratitude *was* a platitude, only more grating.

I flipped the page and started a list of people to thank over the next week, February 1–7. Who would I thank the next day? My mom was an obvious choice, but for what, specifically? How about February 2? Jake? He did just unclog our bathroom toilet. It wouldn't be the most romantic note, but that wasn't the point.

Or maybe I was going about this all wrong. Perhaps I should thank the first person who does something nice for me. I'd be back in Summit the next day. I could thank Cally, who hired me for this consulting gig. Or should I thank the person who makes my lunch? Would that be the cashier who takes my order, or the person who's slicing the lettuce?

This type of scattershot thanking wouldn't work, I recognized. Just as the goal had to be specific—one note for every day of the year—the method had to be as well. If the recipients were randomly selected, I would give up within the month.

Luckily, this problem felt familiar. Magazines, where I had worked for years, are planned out months in advance, on an editorial calendar. I pictured the printed-out spreadsheets that had ruled my life. At *O, The Oprah Magazine*, every month was organized by theme: Age, Power, Gratitude (of course). At *Food & Wine*, there were months dedicated to Travel, Wine, Best New Chefs. Those spreadsheets dedicated a line to each recurring column—for Books That Made a Difference, for 30-Minute Meals—and over time, specific assignments would fill each slot. Planning out columns and features months in advance is how magazines get made, how writing gets done.

I needed to put some structure behind this project. I would make an editorial calendar and fill in every slot. January had been dedicated to charity. I could pick a new topic for February, and another for each month of the year.

I started by jotting down potential themes. What topics were important to me? Friends, of course, and family. Neighbors! My career. Parenting . . . I could thank everyone who'd helped along that crazy journey. That was five topics right there—six, including my already completed charity. I was halfway done.

How about politics? I could thank the politicians and organizers who were fighting for causes I believe in. I would read the newspaper every day, jotting down people who seemed to be . . . Okay. Stop. This felt like homework.

At this point I formed the fundamental rule I lived by all year long: When you spot a potential obstacle—a time suck of any kind that threatens to waylay progress—find a way to knock it down. This project was already ambitious; to complete it, I needed to choose topics that I felt excited about, not ones that felt like a chore, however high-minded and noble.

So what topic *did* excite me? A word sprang to mind: food. *Of course*, I thought, amused. *I could find a way to work food into any project.* Would I write the notes to actual foods—mozzarella and pasta and ice cream? As entertaining a writing prompt as that might be, no. I needed to write to the people behind my favorite foods. And then, travel. I could thank people who enhanced the trips I had loved. And books! I could thank the authors who wrote my most beloved books.

Speaking of my beloved: Jake. Sure, I could lump him into my family section, but maybe he deserved his own month? He was turning forty in December. A card a day could be part of his birthday gift.

I needed only two more topics. What else was important to me? These final ideas came to me in a pair: home and health. Both were fundamental to happiness.

And there you have it: I would write to friends, family members, and neighbors. I would rekindle my love for books, travel, and food. I would honor my home, my health, my husband. I would thank the people who helped me in my parenthood journey and on my career path.

I surveyed the list of themes and felt something click into place. I was adding order to my inner life—mapping my innermost self and forming a plan to reconnect with the parts that were disconnected. I was capturing the confetti.

As for the last item on my list of motivations—*See what good things come of it*—I wondered what would happen when I started putting gratitude into the world. What benefits would I feel? What surprises would come my way? Would I learn any lessons? And would the short-term joy I felt while writing each note lead to a boost in my overall happiness?

I would start close to home, I decided as my train pulled into Penn Station. The next day I would start writing to my neighbors.

HOW TO PLAN A THANK YOU YEAR

Identifying twelve themes is an act of self-love: You are taking yourself seriously enough to think about what's most important to you.

1. *Brainstorm topics.* Feel free to start with some of mine, such as friends, family, neighbors, or career mentors. But really, what matters is you. Ask yourself: What do I love? Which hobbies or habits are important to me? Which memories do I want to revisit? Set a timer for five minutes, and write down your initial ideas.

2. *Choose twelve.* Underline the options that feel the most solid, where potential recipients are already coming to mind. Ask yourself if any of the topics come from an obligatory place. If it sounds like a chore, cross it out.

3. *Refine your topics.* Inspect your underlined themes and think about whether you'd like to keep them broad (theater, music, travel), more specific (Sondheim musicals, jazz concerts, Italy trips), or a mix of both. Look at your emerging list of categories. Is it starting to feel like a blueprint of your inner life? Is anything missing?

4. *Assign topics to months.* Think about what you might be in the mood to focus on at different times of the year. I dedicated my summer months to lighter topics—food, travel—and turned to the more serious task of thanking my career mentors in September. I figured November would be a good time to write to my family members, as I'd be seeing many of them around Thanksgiving anyway.

5. *Stay flexible.* Remember that this list is only an outline. It's meant to be fleshed out, revisited, and updated throughout the year.

CHAPTER TWO

FEBRUARY: NEIGHBORS

How Writing Notes to Neighbors Can Solidify Your Place in the Community

LESSON: Low-stakes relationships can be high-impact.

SURPRISE: Big little favors are happening right now.

BENEFIT: Expressing gratitude forges a deeper connection to the community.

I opted to start with neighbors because I figured it would be the easiest. Neighbors were all around me, literally, so the list would surely come together quickly. And the messages I'd write would be straightforward, short, sweet. Plus, I didn't have to worry about finding addresses or buying stamps: I'd simply hand these over. There would be no complex emotions to convey, no long-lost teachers or friends to track down.

I live in Brooklyn's Carroll Gardens, a tapestry of old school (century-old Italian bakeries, butchers, and cobblers) and new (Pilates studios, tattooed barbers, nationally ranked cocktail lounges). My journalist friend Peter heard on NPR that our neighborhood has more toddlers per capita than anywhere else in America. While facing down oncoming stroller traffic on the brownstone-lined sidewalks, you believe it. In September, the streets close down one by one for bouncy-house block parties; in October, massive inflated spiders cling to the roofs. Sure, our neighborhood has its annoyances. The grocery store prices are brazenly high. Our favorite restaurants are jam-packed even on a frigid Tuesday night in February. At the playground you have to keep an eye out for both rats and rat poison. But overall this was my Mayberry, with mozzarella.

On February 1, it was raining as I walked down Clinton Street while considering which neighbors to thank. I passed our old apartment building and waved to the woman who lived downstairs. While walking past Henry's school I thought of the class parents and raced home to start a list of neighbors in our sphere. My pen could barely keep up. After nearly ten years in the neighborhood, we can't walk to the park without running into at least one person we know. Sometimes we cajole the boys out of the house by making bets on which neighbor we'll see.

Of my list of forty or so people, I would need to winnow it down to twenty-eight, I thought, one for each day of February. I guessed I would just . . . cross out the neighbors I . . . liked the least? Or inversely, star my favorites? My pen hovered over the page. It didn't feel right. A gratitude campaign shouldn't function like a popularity contest.

I gave up on narrowing the list for the moment and instead imagined what I would write, choosing our old downstairs neighbor as an example. Thank you for . . . waving when you see us?

The notes were meant to be simple, but they shouldn't be simplistic; they should have a *little* meat on their bones. Maybe this month wasn't going to be as easy as I'd imagined.

I thought back to my days as a magazine editor, when I had trouble populating columns: 10 Best Dishes in a City, or Travel 101. When a column became difficult to fill—when no city was calling out to have their ten best dishes profiled, when travel tips ran dry—I knew the column had run its course. I needed to think up a new one, and the more specific the parameters were, the stronger the column would be.

Maybe "neighbors" was too vague. Just as my Thank You Year needed an editorial calendar, February required parameters to help me decide which neighbors to thank and what to say.

I meditated on the word "neighbor" and what it meant to be "neighborly." The word evoked a perhaps outdated image of someone popping by with a plate of cookies, encouraging you to drop by if you ever need a cup of sugar.

Some people still had that neighborly instinct, despite chain stores and Amazon Prime. I thought of Marcie, the founder of my Brooklyn businesswomen's networking group, who lent us a folding table for Christmas dinner and insisted on dropping it off and picking it up. Jake and I referred to her throughout the season as "The Woman Who Saved Christmas."

We no longer require our neighbors' muscle to raise our barn, so when someone lends a hand—or a table—it stands out all the more. I decided to write to the people in my community who had displayed generosity to me or my family. That would become the content of the notes—acknowledging those big little favors and explaining how it felt to be on the receiving end.

Low-Stakes Relationships Can Be High-Impact

After writing to Marcie, I thought about the store owners and staff who had shown me generosity. Emma and Michael, who run our favorite bookstore, saw Henry and me peering into the window one morning. "Dancing to *Mary Poppins* in your store before it opened was a highlight of Henry's young life," I wrote. "Thank you for that, and

for opening Books Are Magic, a place where we feel so at home. P.S. I am writing this with a Books Are Magic pen!"

As I turned to our favorite Italian food stores, it quickly became clear that while we loved the freshly made mozzarella, ravioli, rice balls, and eggplant parm, delicious food was not the only reason we visited. We went out of our way to go to Caputo's because of Gianluca. "Thank you for always being so kind & friendly to me and my kids," I wrote to him. "Shopping at Caputo's, or the 'mozz-a-YA-YA store,' is often the best part of our week, thanks in no small part to you."

Esposito's Pork Store is guarded by a statue of a five-foot-tall pig in an apron; inside, it's redolent with the exact smell that once wafted from my grandmother's kitchen in Queens. The first time I walked into Esposito's, the nostalgic scent of simmering tomato sauce, heavy on the onions, brought me to tears. (Here's where Jake would point out that it doesn't take much.) You can't go into Esposito's, or "Espo's," as we call it, when you're in a hurry. Inevitably the person ahead of you in line will strike up a conversation with one of the two Esposito brothers—about the Yankees or marinara ingredients or whichever holiday is coming up. That moment always leaves me feeling jealous, like I'm on the outside looking into this idyllic neighborhood moment. I hoped that writing to both Esposito brothers—who had gifted me rice balls and made me fresh chicken soup—would help me achieve that chummy status.

I had bonded with Alex, the owner of Cantine coffee shop, early one morning when I'd thrown open the door, desperate after breaking my glass coffeemaker. My dad and his partner, Haydee, were in town, and everyone needed coffee—bad. Alex saw the look on my face when she told me they weren't open yet, then poured me huge cups of coffee without charging me. I wrote to her, "You could tell it was an emergency! That meant a lot."

I wanted to thank the neighbors who demonstrated small but important kindnesses that, little by little, made me feel as though I was a part of the fabric of this corner of New York City.

As I wrote to them, that now-familiar calming, meditative focus came over me. But this time I felt something else, too, something new. The notes I'd written in January were explicitly promised to my City Harvest fundraiser donors. The cards for neighbors were just the opposite: unexpected, with a random-act-of-kindness aspect to them. As I finished up, I felt a little thrill, like I had a secret. Actually, I had eleven of them—signed, sealed, and soon to be delivered.

At this stage, I paused. *What if Gianluca thinks this is weird*, I thought, *and our visits become awkward? Is Marcie going to think I'm hopelessly uncool?* But I recognized that even the worst outcome couldn't be too dire.

Besides, as I later found out, those fears of awkwardness are unfounded. Social scientists have spent a lot of time proving that reaching out to connect with a stranger (this chapter, page 24) or to write a friend a letter of gratitude (chapters 7 and 13, pages 98 and 186, respectively) will be far less awkward, and mean a lot more to the recipient, than you can imagine.

I kept the notes tucked in my backpack, and I'd reach for them as I walked past Books Are Magic, Caputo's, Esposito's Pork Store, and Cantine. I rehearsed what I would say as I handed over the card. It went something like—get ready to be dazzled—"Hey! I wrote you a little note; here it is."

I planned to downplay the gesture in person and let the sentimentality come across in the note. Turns out, I didn't have to deliver this well-rehearsed line, as the recipients were rarely at their stores when I dropped by. So that piece became even easier: "This note is for Emma and Michael—can I leave it with you?" It was as simple as that.

The reactions were almost immediate. Emma texted this message: "You are the nicest woman in the world." (Reader: I am not. I asked Jake for an example of my less-nice qualities, and he rattled off three. No need to go into details here.) The next time I stopped by Caputo's, Gianluca came out from behind the counter to give me a hug and ask if I was moving. "That card made me all emotional," he said.

Our conversation stayed with me throughout the day and for weeks afterward. Even now, recounting it a year later, I have a smile on my face. My gratitude project had just begun, and already I was feeling happiness in three stages—from the meditative contentment while writing the notes, to the thrill of delivering them to unsuspecting recipients, to the joy of hearing their reactions.

And these weren't even people in my inner circle. They were people in my *outer* circle. I was taken aback at how happy it made me to connect with them.

To learn more, I reached out to Gillian Sandstrom, the co-author of a study about the importance of "weak ties," or acquaintances. She gave 111 people mechanical clickers to track weak-tie and strong-tie interactions over six days. The participants who reported more daily weak-tie interactions than others reported feeling happier, with a greater sense of belonging.

I asked Sandstrom why interactions with friendly faces (who aren't really friends) matter so much. She started by explaining why social relationships in general matter to us and offered five main reasons: They provide positive stimulation, fun, social comparison, emotional support, and the feeling of being admired and respected.

"Our weak ties can provide stimulation," she pointed out. "We might learn something from them, because they are different from us. They can be fun. So even if they don't provide all of those five things— maybe they are less likely to provide emotional support—they are giving us access to a wider range of social experiences."

That friendly banter with Gianluca and the store owners in the neighborhood? It *meant* something, beyond a pleasant feeling in the moment. It was filling a human need for connection and stimulation. These relationships are significant. On the days when I am hustling, with no time to connect with a friend and barely a moment to talk with Jake on the phone (so, most days), it's nice to know that these quick interactions count as social relationships, providing an accumulation of small bursts of satisfaction and happiness—for me and for them.

"We have strong ties, and they matter the most," Sandstrom said. "But they are a lot of work. Weak ties are not going to be able to fill your needs in the same way as someone close to you can, but they go a long way in helping us feel okay about things."

She explained the origin of the term "weak ties." It came from a 1973 study by Mark Granovetter of Stanford, who found that people are more likely to find a new job through weak ties than through strong ties. "Strong ties know all the same people, so they aren't as helpful as weak ties, who expose you to a wider range of information," Sandstrom explained. "I think that's one of the big benefits. We aren't surprised that often. You're more likely to be surprised by someone you don't know than someone you do know."

Surprise is the flip side of the will-this-be-awkward coin. "Often the 'I don't know what's going to happen' that prevents people from having conversations with strangers turns out in a good way, rather than a bad way," Sandstrom said. She told me about a study in which Nicholas Epley and Juliana Schroeder at the University of Chicago instructed participants to talk to a stranger on their morning commute. Participants reported a more positive experience when they connected than when they didn't. Epley's poetic way of explaining this: "Nobody waves, but everybody waves back."

Sandstrom told me, "You're being the person who waves, and we need those people."

Since conducting her weak ties study in 2014, Sandstrom has turned her attention to talking to strangers: She's trying to understand what people are worried about and how to make it easier for them. "I spend a lot of time teaching people to start conversations," she said. "People want to connect, but they don't exactly know how. That's why we end up sticking to the weather. By writing these thank you notes, maybe you gave people a way to start a conversation that can go a little deeper."

It was true. The notes opened a door that ultimately upgraded my relationships. Marcie and I recently caught up over coffee at a bakery. Alex of Cantine invited me to a regulars' happy hour. I was already friends with Emma, the bookshop owner, but since that *Mary Poppins* morning, our friendship has deepened—she sat across from me at an intimate birthday lunch.

You never know what will happen when you wave first.

Big Little Favors Are Happening Right Now

After delivering the first batch of eleven notes, I walked down Court Street, past a few beloved restaurants, trying to think up more neighbors to thank. No memories came straight to mind, but I trusted that they would.

Over the next few days, as I attempted to retrieve memories, a funny thing started happening: I became aware of kindnesses occurring in real time. There was the neighbor who took pity on me as I tried to park my car. "I hope this is your house!" I wrote. "Thank you so much for parallel parking my car, and for being so nice about it. I'm starting to drive again after a twenty-year break, and I'm easily unnerved."

There was the shuttle bus driver who spotted me running toward him: "Thank you for waiting for me while I ran to make the shuttle—and thank you for being a friendly face in the morning."

There was the Trader Joe's cashier who chased me down the

street: "Thank you for following me out of the store and across Atlantic to return the bag of groceries I forgot. It saved me a lot of trouble, and I really appreciate it!"

I would have noticed these moments regardless—but they would have been passing thoughts. Because I was on the lookout for reasons to write thank you notes, I was able to solidify those fleeting thoughts into grateful sensations, extend the happy feelings while I wrote and delivered the notes, and pass that positivity to the people who started it.

On the day I delivered the thank you card to the cashier at Trader Joe's, my mother-in-law, Lu, arrived bearing salmon patties for dinner and a new winter jacket for Henry. Kindnesses were all around me—not only in my neighborhood but also in my home.

Lu lives in Manhattan and is not a neighbor, technically speaking. But it felt wrong to thank the Trader Joe's cashier for six minutes of his time without acknowledging Lu for hours of hers. I had every intention of writing to twenty-eight neighbors in February, but what was I going to do, wait to thank Lu until November, my family month, just to adhere to the framework I'd created?

While each month would revolve around a topic, I decided it would be fine, even beneficial, to mix in thank yous for family members and friends.

Besides Lu, in February I thanked my mom for sending clothes for the kids, my dad for mailing a box of oranges and avocados from his yard, his partner and her sister for helping with my kids and the laundry, my sister for bringing us Oaxacan souvenirs, and my brother for "lying on the floor until Henry calmed down and fell asleep."

When seen together like this, over the course of just one month, it became movingly clear how much support I had holding me up—from ties both weak and strong.

Expressing Gratitude Forges a Deeper Connection to the Community

The next time I walked into Esposito's, the cashier called me by my name for the first time. I looked at him curiously. "I know you," he said with a smile, and pointed toward the kitchen. There, taped to the wall, was my note.

Dear John,

> A couple of years ago, I was shopping at Esposito's, pregnant and VERY hungry. I asked for four rice balls, and only had cash for two (I realized once I checked). You not only gave me my order, but threw in two more. Thank you for your generosity and kindness. I've never forgotten it! We're so lucky to have Esposito's in the neighborhood.
>
> Love, Gina

I couldn't stop staring at my name. A piece of me now lived here, in the place that reminded me so much of my grandparents' tomato-scented basement that I once wept because of it. It was as if my name had been sewn into my neighborhood's tapestry.

HOW TO THANK YOUR NEIGHBORS

1. *Come up with a number.* It doesn't need to be twenty-eight or thirty. Even if it's four—one per week—it's useful to choose a number to hit. The goal means that you'll inevitably think of people who weren't obvious choices and who might turn out to be the most interesting or rewarding of the bunch.

2. *Set parameters.* It sounds counterintuitive, but strict boundaries breed creativity. I chose "neighbors who have done me a favor."

3. *Keep your eyes open.* In addition to retrieving memories, be aware of kindnesses happening in real time.

4. *Go off topic.* As you get into the practice of acknowledging big little favors, you're likely to spot them coming from all directions, not just from neighbors but also from friends, coworkers, family members. Go on, thank them. You need to hit that number, after all.

5. *Snap a picture.* Get into the habit of documenting the notes you're writing. At the end of the year, it'll be nice to look back on all the gratitude you've expressed.

6. *Deliver the notes.* Don't overthink what to say—let the note speak for itself.

CHAPTER THREE

MARCH: FRIENDS

How Writing "Remember When?" Postcards Reestablishes Bonds and Heals Wounds

LESSON: Nostalgia can be sent by mail.

BENEFIT: Thanking old friends can be cathartic.

SURPRISE: Long-lost friends aren't always lost.

After spending February recognizing and reinforcing connections close to home, I decided to dedicate March to friends who live farther afield.

As I sat down to write up a list of recipients, I knew one parameter right off the bat. At the top of a page I wrote, "Friends Who I Miss (aka not in NYC)." Having grown up in California and attended school in Michigan, I came up with plenty of names.

The challenge arose when I imagined what the notes would say. First, I tried using the structure that worked for my neighbors month, attempting to remember a time when they had gone above and beyond. But it felt odd to imagine thanking my friend Kristy for teaching me how to straighten my hair in 1999. I didn't want to assign myself that chore, retrieving decades-old memories of favors big and small.

Besides, friendship isn't about favors. I wanted to thank my friends simply for being themselves. But if I simply wrote that out—*thank you for being a friend*—well, I would be plagiarizing the *Golden Girls* theme song without attribution. More to the point, the notes would either be short and generic (*Thank you for your friendship, I love you*) or long and rambling, as I attempted to encapsulate everything each person meant to me.

While puzzling this out, I opened a box of photographs, hoping it would lend clues. At the top was a picture from my last visit to my hometown, Palos Verdes, California, a peninsula on the southern tip of Los Angeles County. My friend Katrina—BFF from sixth grade on—had hosted a party for my younger son Charlie's first birthday. There are six of us girls in her driveway, with Katrina's homemade felt streamers in the background. We are laughing, holding on to our wriggly kids as best as we can. My heart felt so full that day.

In my smile I recognized relief: My old friends were still my friends. We might not spend the day getting sunburned on the beach or the night skinny dipping in the waves, as we did in high school. We don't climb the hidden path to the landing carved out of the Lunada Bay cliffs to smoke cigarettes. We are no longer teenagers without fears of cancer or riptides or slippery cliffs. We aren't kids—we have our kids to tend to. Every annual visit is one more year past those carefree days. I worried, as the stretches between visits became longer and longer, the memories hazier, that I was losing these friends.

Deeper in the shoe box were pictures of that same group of

girls—as bridesmaids at one another's weddings and, deeper still, as tiny fourteen-year-olds, string-bikini ties peeking out of tie-dyed shirts. There were shots of my college friends in short, shaggy haircuts and raisin-colored lipstick. Before I knew it, more than an hour had passed—shoe boxes of photos are the pre-internet Instagram—and I felt aglow with nostalgia. That feeling, that warmth—*that* is what I wanted to convey in the notes. But how?

I suddenly remembered that photographs could be sent as post-cards. And I had ten sheets of postcard stamps that I needed to use, due to a late-night ordering snafu.

These pictures were growing yellow and warped. Wouldn't a few of them be put to better use as instruments of my gratitude?

Nostalgia Can Be Sent by Mail

I knew about the picture-as-postcard trick thanks to my former boss Maile Carpenter, who used to send photographs wrapped in cellophane for her holiday cards. I emailed her for advice, and she responded right away: "Funny you remembered that! We used to Cryovac our photo and put a stamp on it, but you can do the same with four-by-six resealable cellophane bags . . . like these." Helpfully, she included a link to buy the clear plastic envelopes. While I was on the store website, I threw in four-by-six mailing labels and pens that can write directly onto photographs. (Internet searching led me to Staedtler Lumocolor universal pens.)

A few days later, armed with all my supplies, I did a test run. With those special pens, I wrote a sample message directly on the back of a four-by-six photo, and I inserted it into a clear cellophane envelope. It was a squeeze, and I ripped the seam of three envelopes before the picture slid in.

I also tried slapping a four-by-six shipping label onto the back of a four-by-six photo, folding the label overhang over the picture. Not terribly neat, but it did the job.

I took both prototypes to our local mailing center, Cobble Hill Variety Mailing on Henry Street, where the friendly owner, Omar, inspected my handiwork and deemed the cruder shipping label option the winner, pointing out that while the cellophane protected the picture, it was flimsy and would likely get bent in transit.

Did Omar get a thank you note? You can bet your weak ties on it.

Logistics settled, I turned back to my photo boxes and chose a stack of twenty-six pictures, allowing for five non-theme thank you cards, including Omar's, to reach my March batch of thirty-one. I affixed the labels and drew vertical lines to make space for the addresses and shell-embossed postcard stamps (each one 18 cents less than regular postage, score!).

On the train to New Jersey the next morning, I shuffled my post-cards and selected a picture of me and my friend Molly from our semester abroad.

I took a breath, cleared out all other thoughts and distractions, and focused on the picture. I wrote: "Oh man, there was a time when you lived in Amsterdam and I lived in Italy, and we were entirely care-free. Did we appreciate it? We were eating ice cream, so that's a start. Miss the days I could spend hanging with you, and MISS YOU! I'm so grateful for our years of friendship, and I'm so grateful to know you."

Next up was a picture of my college roommate Alison sitting on a motor scooter, me in a helmet smiling beside her. I am betraying none of the crippling fear or adrenaline I was feeling just before riding a scooter on the rural roads of Portugal. Indeed, later that day I ended up skidding and falling as we pulled into a parking lot. "This picture makes me laugh," I wrote. "I look like I know what I'm doing, right?

Looking through old pictures, I found so many of the two of us. So grateful for our years of friendship. Miss and love you—and can't wait for the next time we get to sit and catch up."

The notes flowed fast and easy now that I had something to write about—the picture, and the memories it brought up.

As I got into the zone, by instinct I started templating the beginning and then adding personalized details. A template, in magazine terms, is a column or article that's structured the same way in every issue. It's a way into a topic that is simultaneously idiosyncratic and predictable and, because you're not reinventing the wheel each month, easier to produce.

Think about the back page of magazines. Here is a random selection from publications I've worked at (and, therefore, have handy in a cupboard): Celeb Fridge, a peek inside a famous person's refrigerator (*Rachael Ray Every Day*); What I Know for Sure, an essay by Oprah (*O*); If I Were President, a Q&A with a celebrity (*George*); Most Wanted, a chef's most requested recipe (*Food & Wine*).

My postcard template began with the phrase "Remember when we were young and carefree . . . ?" That opener captured what I missed from past decades more than anything else—long, luxurious stretches of time with my friends.

To Liz, sitting in the Piazza del Campo in Siena: "Remember when we were young and carefree and getting to know each other in Italy? Don't tell Jake, but I don't think anyone makes me laugh as hard as you do. As Maggie wrote in the winery guest book: THANK YOU FOR THE FRIENDSHIP."

To Megan: "Remember when we were in our carefree twenties and looked like American Apparel models? I miss those days and I miss YOU! Thank you for being your funny, smart, wonderful self, and thank you for being my friend."

I wrote three separate postcards to my BFF Katrina, the one who hosted Charlie's first birthday party, documenting three stages of our friendship—when we were eleven, sixteen, and twenty-two—because I found so many incredible pictures of us that I couldn't pick just one.

Once I completed fifteen or so postcards, I gathered addresses via text, keeping the reason vague. ("I have a little note to send you!") I found my long-dormant sky-blue address book and started updating it, anticipating all the note-writing in the year ahead.

Even the straightforward task of gathering addresses elicited bit-

tersweet emotions. When my high school friend Paige sent me her address, I typed it into Google Street View. It was strange, first of all because I never imagined this project would include anything from the stalker play-book, but mostly because this person with whom I had spent countless hours lived in a house I'd never visited. Her kids' pictures popped up on my phone, but I'd never walked through that white fence and under that trellis to the front door.

I inspected the completed postcards, and wondered what each of these friends might be doing at that moment. I imagined a massive Marauder's Map alight with activity, showing each of their footprints puttering around in their homes, going from room to room.

As I sent the cards off to houses I've never seen in California and Seattle and Chicago, I thought about how keeping old friendships alive took time, and that time was something we once had but no longer do.

When time becomes scarce, why is friendship the first thing to be sacrificed? Maybe it explains social media's skyrocketing rise: We are all craving the friendships we had when we were younger, and we settle for this faux version because it's all we think we have time for. This month's correspondence took a little effort and time, to be sure—but it meant more than a social media smiley face, and it was more efficient than scheduling twenty-six catch-up phone calls.

Who knows when those will happen? It could be years. Until then, I wanted to send these people my love and gratitude for our friendship, and I hoped that the gesture acted as a bookmark until we are able to sit down, face-to-face.

The replies started coming fast, mostly via the *ping* of texts showing note-holding selfies. "I've been looking at this picture of us every day and it makes me smile." "You made my day!!!!" "Your postcard made me cry and made my day!!!!" "Your postcard made my week. Inspired me to send a nice note to an old friend as well!" I also listened to some heartstring-tugging voicemails.

Effusive reactions were never my motivation. In early February, I wrote this Thank You Year directive in my notebook: "Give everything. Expect nothing. Don't keep track of responses. Keep them, but never go back to the list to check or follow up."

That said, these replies felt pretty wonderful. Hearing that I made my friends' days made *my* day, week, and beyond.

Thanking Old Friends Can Be Cathartic

Warmth and nostalgia gave way to anxiety and wariness as I reached the bottom of the postcard stack. There were four cards that I kept shuffling to the bottom of the deck, and soon I would run out of other notes and excuses and have to actually write them.

I wrote in my notebook, "What about the people I've lost touch with who once meant so much?" My relationships with these four were situated somewhere on a spectrum between "not the same" and "estranged."

For the first time, I worried about how a note would be received. In my neighbors month, I had brushed aside any brief hesitation or fear of awkwardness. The stakes were low, and in the event of rejection, I didn't have much to lose. Now the stakes felt real. Would this postcard come across as glib? Would my note read as passive-aggressive? Why was I doing this, anyway? Was it to reach my quota of thirty-one people to thank in March, or was it for more noble reasons—specifically, to open a door? Was a postcard the right way to do that?

I started with the easiest of the four. Catherine was my dearest friend in college, but we'd grown apart in the intervening years. In the picture, we were on a Ferris wheel car hovering above the blue water of Lake Michigan. "Oh man, how cute & carefree are we?" I wrote. "I want you to know that though we aren't in close contact, I will forever be grateful for your friendship. You were my absolute touchstone during our college years, and that connection was so important."

Jon and I met while studying in Florence, and he became one of my closest friends when we were living in New York in our twenties: He was in my bridal party as the lone "bridesman." The waters were muddied after he and my sister, Brigitte, fell in love, moved in together, and eventually broke up. We saw each other maybe once a year, when he was back in town from the West Coast, but it wasn't the same. In the picture, he and I and two friends are standing in a group hug in front of the Colosseum in Rome. To him, I wrote: "Oh man—remember when we were young & carefree & staying in disgusting hostels & having an absolute ball? Miss those days & miss you. So grateful for our years of friendship, Jon."

Vijay was my confidant in high school, and we stayed close through college. We'd last seen each other in my neighborhood seven or eight years ago; the dinner felt strained somehow, and we hadn't spoken since. In the picture Vijay is wearing a Hawaiian-print tie and suspenders, looking dapper for my sorority formal. "Remember when we were young & talked for hours at a time on the phone? The best. Thank you for being a dear friend when I really needed one. Though we aren't in touch right now, with all of life's busyness, I hope to be in the future."

Revisiting the starting point of these relationships and sitting with my complicated feelings about how they'd evolved or devolved over time forced me to process complex feelings—frustration, sadness, loss. But writing the words was cathartic. I felt a release: My shoulders relaxed as I wrote.

I don't know what Catherine, Jon, or Vijay imagined when I emailed them to ask for their addresses. I know I felt scared and nervous standing at the mailbox on my street corner. But I had come this far—here went nothing.

Within a week I had responses from all three. Catherine texted, "You have a special place in my heart always." Jon told me he missed me in an email with the subject line "That was so thoughtful." And Vijay wrote a long email from Chicago, where he has set the note prominently on his desk, saying that he often thinks "back to that time in high school" and feels "very grateful about having you as a friend. You definitely made a big difference in my life."

Those responses got me thinking about the phrase "lost touch," which is rather poetic. Was our *touch* something that had simply been misplaced? What if it could be regained by something as simple as a postcard?

My gratification was tempered by the month's final task. I had one more postcard left to write, and this one would be the toughest. Sara didn't fit my thank you note parameter: She lived in Brooklyn. She wasn't far away physically, but she was far away emotionally. We hadn't been in contact in years. She came to my baby shower and then fell away from my life. It felt like she dumped me when I was about to become a mother, when our lifestyles were about to diverge.

In the picture I am hugging her from behind and our faces are close together. Our friendship was the most meaningful one I made in my twenties. I admired the courageous, artistic way she moved through the world. She was the lead singer and songwriter in a band. She took me to museum exhibits and gallery openings. She introduced me to her impossibly fashionable and fascinating group of friends. We had an easy rapport from the start. We'd lose entire afternoons to conversations about books and family dramas—she was an excellent amateur shrink. We had met once in the past five years: She'd reached out to tell me she was pregnant. But then she disappeared again. I took a deep breath, focused on the photograph, and started writing.

"Remember when we were carefree and went on NYC adventures? Befriending you was unlocking a door to a magical city of rosé, art, music . . . and I'm so grateful. I miss our long, luxurious talks & brunches, but excited to catch up the next time."

I felt entirely vulnerable as the postcard went through the mail slot; I actually felt butterflies in my stomach.

Those nerves ramped up when I saw her name in my inbox. "Today amongst all the crappy bed bath and beyond fliers and credit card offers was the sweetest photo and note ever," she wrote. "Oh, how I remember those wonderful carefree days!! We had so much fun, and those long days and nights stretched out in front of us with no cares and no little kiddos to wake us up at 6 in the morning. I'd love to catch up soon. Tell me your schedule? I'll sneak out of work for a few hours and come hang with you? Xxxx."

Long-Lost Friends Aren't Always Lost

Sara sat across from me at the co-working space I'd joined this month. I forced myself to uncross my arms. I could tell she was nervous, too, by the high pitch of her nervous laughter and the way she picked at her nails.

After a few minutes of small talk (the stylishness of the room, the view of the Brooklyn Bridge through the window), Sara launched into what had been going on in her life, recounting that her relationship "exploded" about a year ago, that she had been struggling with motherhood to begin with, and that single motherhood was even harder. She'd been diagnosed with rheumatoid arthritis to boot. "I pull away when I feel like my life is a mess," she said, "because I'm not able to radiate joy or good things."

Her vulnerability disarmed me. As she spoke, what went through my head, aside from feeling sadness and compassion for my friend, were these words, over and over: Maybe it's not about me.

From there, our conversation took on a familiar shape. We talked about her parents in Vermont. She asked about each member of my family, which snowballed into a therapy session and had me rubbing away tears while explaining tensions resulting from a strained weekend with my in-laws. Her specific blend of intelligent listening and sage advising—she helped me come up with talking points—was helpful, as it once had been.

The lunch lasted two hours and morphed into a work date. She helped me organize pictures into a grid for a social media client; I proofread a press release for her upcoming art show. Before saying goodbye, she pulled out a Polaroid that she'd taken at my wedding and held on to for twelve years. In the foreground is me from the elbow down, twirling in my dress; three men are in the background clapping—one is my dad, I think. The picture had movement and playfulness and grace. It was begging to be blown up and framed. I'd mailed her a photograph, and she brought me one in return.

picture postcard

long-lost photo

back-in-touch lunch

We pledged to meet again at the gallery she runs on the Lower East Side—and we kept that date three weeks later. She gave me a tour of the current exhibit, comprising photographs and installations that found levity and beauty in the everyday: breath mints arranged on a tray table; pickup sticks artfully scattered on a platform. We visited another gallery and then browsed a plant store and slurped big bowls of pho. Our dynamic felt the opposite of fraught. It felt *normal*, and I was so grateful.

Soon afterward, in a phone conversation, she explained her reaction to my postcard, which, she told me, was on her fridge. "I avoid my mail like the plague because it's endless credit card bills and nothing fun and nothing good," she said. "So it was surprising to see a picture of you and me on a card. I was like, 'What is this magical thing?' And I turned it over and read it. Thinking of carefree days resonated with me because my life had become the opposite of the life that I had when we met. That picture brought me right back to those happy times. I also remember feeling like, *I have done such a bad job keeping in touch with Gina, and I'm ashamed.* And yet I felt, *Gina still loves me. Even though I haven't been around, and she doesn't know why.* It was a reach over the chasm of my own stuff, across the divide."

I told her that the photo had been hard for me to send. I wasn't sure if it was the right way to reach out, for one thing. How had it felt different from receiving a call or an email? I wondered.

"To start, the picture itself was powerful. Feelings flooded into me. I know when the picture was taken. I remember that joyful time. And then, getting something in the mail is a slow way of communicating, and it allows for a slow process of thinking. At first, I thought, *Oh, this is so nice, and she's so sweet.* And then, *Oh, gosh, I really dropped the ball. Would she want to hear from me?* And then, *I guess she does, because she wrote me this card.* It was a grand gesture, and I could choose to respond in my own way, whatever and whenever that was going to be."

She went on to say, "I was touched that you went to the trouble to make a card, which is more time-consuming than typing out an email or getting on the phone. It has the weight of your effort. In art, we say, 'You can see the hand,' which is the human effort behind something. This bears the mark of the hand."

It was such a beautiful way to put it, and I was reminded of one reason I loved Sara—for her uniquely smart perspective. And I felt melancholy, too, for the time we had missed.

I brought up the origin of our estrangement, how it coincided with my becoming a mother. "I was a mess at your baby shower," she admitted. "I had been dating some guy, and he broke up with me, and I was like, 'Why did I bring my crazy drama to this beautiful baby shower?'"

I told her I had imagined she wasn't interested in being my friend once I had a baby. I could hear her sharp intake of breath. "I understand that idea, and I've had that feeling about people who I felt disappeared once I had my baby. That's not it at all. I felt like I was failing at a lot of things. I've always tried to present a good version of myself to people, and when I'm not able to, I'm not sure what to present."

(Once more, with feeling: Maybe it's not about me.)

She continued: "I'm so sorry. I truly apologize because that wasn't okay as a friend. It's not okay to disappear because you're feeling depressed. Even though I seem like I'm this emotionally fluent person, when I'm truly struggling, I'm not emotionally fluent. I'm miserable inside, and I stay by myself until a point when I can put the words together to share what I'm feeling with other people. It is not a good way to live, and I've had to reconcile with that."

I didn't reach out to Sara looking for an apology, but hearing one went a long way toward healing the wound from the last years.

"Your card coming through the ether to me started a domino effect of us being able to repair our friendship," she said, "and it taught me an amazing lesson: Don't presume that you have disappointed someone so much that they're not going to want to be your friend. Maybe there's room for you to have been disappointing, and then redeem yourself. People fall off the tightrope of their life and get back on. What I'm trying to do is get back on the tightrope, and be a better version of myself."

It was one of the most honest and meaningful conversations I can remember, and we wouldn't have had it—not really, not in such depth—if I weren't writing this book. Why not?

"We talk about how to be an active participant in romantic relationships and how to work on that," Sara pointed out. "We don't give friendships the value they deserve."

Writing my friends' names on a list, finding old pictures of us, and describing how much I missed them, then repairing relationships that were damaged—this was my way of saying that friendship has value. *Your* friendship has incredible value to me. Still.

HOW TO WRITE
"REMEMBER WHEN?"
POSTCARDS

1. *Go through old photos,* whether they're in online files or a shoe box (if you don't have duplicates, you could make copies). Grab (or print) the ones that make you laugh or bring up strong feelings.

2. *Reinforce each photo* with a four-by-six shipping label. If there's overhang, trim it or fold it onto the picture. Draw a vertical line to leave space for the address and postage on the right-hand side. (You've seen a postcard; you get it.)

3. *Clear out all other distractions.* Focus on the person in the picture and that moment in time. What do you remember? How do you feel?

4. *Try starting with the phrase "Remember when?"* and then share the memories and feelings that the picture brings up. You have room for only a couple of sentences—make them honest and specific.

5. *Be kind when reaching out to an estranged friend.* This isn't the place to get into hurt feelings or anger—that's better expressed in conversation. But you shouldn't lie, in words or in tone. There's no need to be perky. Write from the heart what *is* true: what you miss about that person, why you treasure the memories that the picture evokes. Then mail it, and see what happens.

CHAPTER FOUR

APRIL: PARENTING

How Writing Letters to the Village Can  Make for a Happier Parent

LESSON: A good thank you note transcends the transactional.

SURPRISE: Children are gratitude sponges.

BENEFIT: Expressing gratitude can assuage mom guilt.

My "Remember When?" postcards to friends had a fairly straightforward subtext: "Remember life before kids?" While I spent March revisiting and romanticizing those carefree, child-free days, I hoped that the hours spent reflecting on parenting in April would help me savor its wild joys and minimize its frustrations. Maybe it would help me recover some of the sun-dappled magic of the baby years.

Four years prior, I was walking in Cobble Hill Park with Henry strapped to my chest—a tiny baby with giant eyes the exact shade and size of blueberries—when a man stopped me to say, "You must feel like the luckiest woman in the world." About a week later, with Henry in that same carrier, I saw a five- or six-year-old kid slug a woman in a purple sweater and scream, "I'm just so *tired!*" The (assumed) mother turned to me and said, in an almost menacing voice, "Enjoy your baby now. It doesn't get any better."

I had gulped and squeezed Henry a little tighter, gloating just a little about how good we had it. Every day seemed to bring new miracles, and every night I would literally weep with gratitude.

I would start Henry's bedtime routine by reading Nancy Tillman's heartfelt *Wherever You Are, My Love Will Find You*, a gift from my California friend Sam. This is the line that would get me every time: "And if someday you're lonely, or someday you're sad, or you strike out at baseball, or you think you've been bad . . . just lift up your face, feel the wind in your hair. That's me, my sweet baby, my love is right there."

If I managed to keep it together while reading the book, the tears would inevitably flow as I nursed Henry to sleep while singing "In My Life" by the Beatles, generally during the wobbly refrain: *"In my-ah-ah-ay life, I loved you . . . moooooore."*

It had been years since I read Henry *Wherever You Are, My Love Will Find You* or sang him "In My Life." Since he was about two, Henry has insisted on an ever-changing mix of books—*Blueberries for Sal, Mike Mulligan and His Steam Shovel* (charming classics badly in need of an editor)—and kid songs by Raffi and Mister Rogers.

Lately, there was less time to treasure the sweet moments. This month I was extra-slammed planning Henry's fifth birthday party. It was the reason I'd matched the "parenting" topic to April, figuring I'd meet my monthly thank you note quota while acknowledging the gifts Henry had received.

For a birthday party theme, Henry requested "Moana on Broadway." (His initial, ultimately rejected brainchild was "Ninjas on Broadway." Offering up that gem here in case any producers are reading.) We'd recently gone to his first Broadway show, *Frozen*, where he spent 90 percent of the show cowering in the lobby and 10 percent monkey-gripped onto me in the back of the theater.

The party, on the other hand, was a lei-wearing, hula-dancing, beer-drinking (for the grown-ups) success, thanks to hours of planning and decoration ordering. Afterward, as wrapping paper flew into my face, I diligently wrote down his twenty gifts and their givers. I figured I would be done with most of April's thank you notes in a day or two.

A Good Thank You Note Transcends the Transactional

For a week I carried around the handwritten list of thank you recipients and a stack of butterfly-embossed cards. I would pull them out during my train ride, but I kept on reading my engrossing book, *Educated* by Tara Westover. Or I would call Jake to go over weekend plans. Or I would respond to emails. A week became two, which became three, which became the last weekend in April, without even one card to show for the month.

That Saturday afternoon, while Charlie was napping and Jake and Henry were at the park, I sat at my writing desk to face the task. I started tidying and reorganizing and *Oh, my God, why can't I just write these notes?*

It struck me: I hate writing thank you notes! I was dreading the task because it felt like a duty—as writing any traditional, confirmation-of-receipt thank you note does.

I had to rethink the standard form. I would start by thanking the recipient for coming to Henry's party and giving him Legos, toy cars, terrarium kits, rock-painting sets, and the like. Then I challenged myself to go deeper.

I thought about my neighbor friend Sara—different Sara from the one with whom I'd reconnected—and how I'd always admired her mothering approach. She bends down and talks to her children in a soft tone of voice she uses only with them. To her and her husband

I wrote: "Five years into parenthood, I'm feeling sentimental. I want you to know that you two have been some of our parenting role models from the start."

I wrote to more of our neighborhood friends, whom we lean on for last-minute plans and advice. To Anna and Fred: "Thank you mostly for being our go-to hangout friends." And to Mari and Jorma: "We couldn't be more grateful to be doing this parenting thing with you."

To Nick and Ro, who catered our parental leaves with pots of chili and bowls of homemade hummus and trays of brownies, and who shower Henry with attention: "I so appreciate the care and love you've always shown Henry, and the support you've given us as parents. It takes a village indeed . . . and we're so lucky you're in ours!"

These past five years, Jake and I had built a parenting village out of our neighbors and friends. The village's structure was dependent, though, on our family members and caregivers. I wrote to my in-laws, Lu and Andy: "We're so lucky to have you both so close by, and so involved." And I thanked our nanny, Rhonda, for "all the big and small ways you take care of Henry and Charlie. We are so grateful for you. You make our lives possible, and you do your job with a lot of love and care—it really shows."

My siblings have been Henry's biggest fans from the beginning. To my brother, Alex: "Thank you for showing up, babysitting, playing. . . . The kids adore you, and it means so much to me. I'm not sure how I could have managed these five years of parenting without your steadfast support." And to my sister, Brigitte: "The world has never known a more loving, helpful aunt."

And though they live in California, my parents have always found ways to show their love. My mom had sent Henry a Moana doll and Maui shirts to fit the theme, and my dad and his partner had ordered all the Hawaiian decorations. I thanked my brother-in-law and his girlfriend for taking us to Henry's ill-fated yet milestone first Broadway show.

I knew how lucky I was to have a great nanny and helpful friends and family members. But writing to each of them, one by one, and seeing the stack of cards in aggregate, helped me identify and visualize our amorphous parenting village, and it filled me with profound gratitude.

Children Are Gratitude Sponges

I still had to thank Henry's classmates for their gifts. I started each card by dutifully noting each toy or puzzle, and then asked Henry to dictate a special message. Complimenting friends (and strangers on the street) comes naturally to Henry, so he took to this task right away: "I love to hug you." "I think you're super funny, sweet, and kind." "You are always silly at lunchtime, and I like that."

Since adding his trademark food pairings to January's thank you notes, Henry had been pitching in where he could. He helped to deliver some of February's notes to neighborhood friends, including our shuttle bus driver.

He's been a recipient, too: I wrote him a card after he accidentally ripped my childhood Raggedy Ann doll and asked his grandmother Lu to fix it. "You know that Annie was so special to me when I was your age, and the fact that you thought of fixing her and doing something about it means a lot to me. You have such a big heart, honey." Henry asked me to read the note to him three times in a row.

As we walked to school in the mornings, Henry liked to ask, "Are you writing any thank you notes today? Tell me what you're going to write." He became my cheerleader, telling me that the project was "awesome" and offering up a frequent "Good job, Mommy!"

It was around this time, right after he turned five, that Henry started employing a new phrase: "I'm grateful for you." First, he said it to me and Jake and Charlie, and then he spread it far and wide: to his teachers, to his best friend, Aurelia, and her mom, Stephanie, to name a few examples. As I write this, a year and a half later, Henry continues to say it regularly.

Henry started getting more specific with his gratitude as well. "I love this pea soup! Thank you for cooking it for me, Mommy!" And, at his special sushi birthday lunch: "This softshell crab is delicious! Thank you for making it," he said to the chef, and then turned to me and suggested we write him a thank you note. (Something *I'm* grateful for is Henry's adventurous palate. Charlie, on the other hand, is suspicious of any food that's not mac and cheese.)

Henry was not only feeling gratitude frequently, he was feeling it deeply. During the Passover seder, he stood up to make an announcement: "Excuse me, everyone. You're all being very polite, and I appreciate it. I am grateful for you all!"

And during the 2020 shutdown, Henry concluded a homework recording to his teacher by saying, "In this difficult time with the virus, I want you to know, Ms. Bruno, that you are doing a great job. Thank you for everything you're doing."

Henry was born a sweet and affectionate kid—one with a talent for needling his parents, more on that later—but his focus on gratitude was something new, and it stemmed directly from this project. I wondered, Are all children as receptive to gratitude? Yes, according to the psychology professors Jeffrey Froh and Giacomo Bono, who wrote the 2014 book *Making Grateful Kids.*

Dispersed throughout the book are thirty strategies for teaching kids to be grateful, and as I read through it I realized how many were tactics I'd been implementing that year: modeling gratitude, for one thing, and encouraging grateful thinking by pointing out good things that were happening and the people responsible for them.

"Attributing people responsible for the good things in our life is one of the most important connections, in terms of a child's development," Bono told me over the phone, and he agreed that watching me express gratitude was influential to Henry. "He saw that this is something that's important to you, and he listened when you explained why. People ask me all the time, what's the trick to making grateful kids? And I always say, lots of conversations."

While researching the book, Bono and his co-author conducted a study in a New York State elementary school, dividing 120 fourth graders into a test group and a control group. The test group underwent a gratitude curriculum: Every day for one week they learned about a hypothetical situation in which students imagined themselves as the protagonist in a story that had a benefactor, like a sister or a friend. Lesson plans included understanding the benefactor's intention and the personal cost to them.

Students who received the gratitude curriculum reported more grateful thinking, and their teachers rated them as happier overall than the control group. These findings held true in a longer study that was spread out over five weeks. I wondered, though, whether one or even five weeks was enough time. It took Henry months of gratitude exposure before I saw a change in him.

The authors also organized a school-wide presentation about gratitude that ended with a thinly veiled moral choice: "The presentation you just saw was given by our Parent-Teacher Association. We have about five minutes of free time. You can use the time to write a thank you card to the PTA using the paper provided, or you can just hang out."

"Ha!" I wrote in my notes, finding that choice a touch leading. *Do the right thing, kids!* Students who had been experiencing the gratitude curriculum wrote 80 percent more thank you notes to the PTA than students in the control group, which Bono and his co-author claimed "provided external validation of the findings," and evidence that "intervention focused on increasing gratitude actually leads to behavioral changes." I wasn't convinced: Wouldn't the notes have been more meaningful if written to a teacher or parent or friend? How do you write a heartfelt card to the faceless PTA?

But Bono had more recent evidence to share. He was excited to tell me about a classroom app called GiveThx, which he had co-launched along with a high school teacher in Oakland, California. The app, now being used in more than eighty schools around the country, allows students to ping messages of thanks to their peers in a way that's simple and private (read: not embarrassing) yet impactful. The messages have tags (friendship, generosity, courage, listening) that allow them to be graphed, so students can start to see a pattern: They've been thanked mostly for their kindness and compassion, say, and are usually thanking others for their encouragement and help.

Bono said that the results have been incredible: Classrooms that use the app are reporting improved moods and mental health, as well as lower anxiety and depression and stress.

"It turns out that the best practices outlined in our book's gratitude curriculum weren't enough," Bono said. "The opportunity to practice and say thank you autonomously is key. When the curriculum and the app are *both* in use, that seems to be producing the impact that we'd hoped for."

In other words, he was saying what I'd been discovering for myself: Benefits really start rolling in when you take the gratitude you are feeling and share it with the people responsible.

Expressing Gratitude Can Assuage Mom Guilt

As I was wrapping up my notes for the month, I wanted to write two to Henry and Charlie, and planned to do so after spending a day together.

The day was horrible. I don't remember the details. I imagine that

I asked Henry to stop doing something—let's say, throwing a bouncy ball at the bookshelf near breakable framed pictures—and he continued to do that thing while staring me dead in the eyes. And he probably left the gate at the top of the stairs open and ready for his twenty-one-month-old brother to tumble down, despite my reminding him six or seven times—that hour. Most likely he refused to clean up any of the Legos scattered like so much confetti. By the end of the day I likely had the feeling that the kids were taking pieces from me until there was nothing left. I probably called Jake at some point to say, "Motherhood is death by a thousand cuts."

The only concrete detail I remember is crying in the laundry room while listening to Joni Mitchell sing, "I wish I had a river I could skate away on."

It wasn't the ideal evening to compose thank you notes to my children. But after bedtime I stuck to the plan and sat down to write. (This is where my goal-oriented side can get a little out of hand.) When I was done, I read over the notes, which sounded passive-aggressive, like those venting emails you draft to your boss but never send. Especially the one to Henry.

Despite his sweet nature and proclamations of gratitude, Henry had been pushing my buttons since Charlie was born. Henry adored Charlie from the start and thankfully never took his "What about me?" feelings out on him. He saved them all for me. For months, Henry insisted on eating every meal while sitting on my lap—spilling most of his food so that I was covered not only in breast milk but also jam and soggy Cheerios. He came upstairs one morning to find me nursing Charlie in bed and threw a tantrum.

"Charlie gets breakfast in bed?" he asked. "I want breakfast in bed! Stop laughing!"

It was a funny story, one that Jake and I liked to tell, but looking back now I see how desperate Henry was for my attention—and it seemed like I could never shine enough on him. "Bad attention" became a phrase we used a lot—as in, please, Henry, don't go after bad attention.

As I looked at my botched thank you note attempt, I felt defeated. Had I turned into that woman on the sidewalk in the purple sweater? At least Henry hadn't physically assaulted me. Yet.

I felt guilty and angry at myself—for failing to steer the day in a better direction, to help Henry through our transition into a family of four, to be a more patient and lighthearted mother, to muster enough gratitude to write a decent thank you note to my kindhearted son.

"Dear Henry." I touched the beginning words of the note and remembered something. In my early thirties I had written about a dozen letters to my future child, starting when I couldn't wait to become a mother and continuing for the first few months of Henry's life.

"Dear You," I had written at the start of each note. I told my future child about the last birth control pill I took, in the spring of 2011, when the cherry tree was in bloom outside the window of our home office ("your bedroom soon"). In April 2012 I wrote about the Chinese herbs I was forcing down while struggling to get pregnant, writing, "I thought I'd be holding you in my arms right about now, but that's okay. We are waiting for exactly you." In September 2012 I wrote about the day I finally found out I was pregnant and was "floating in a happy little dream state." I ended that note with "You're barely the size of a poppy seed, and already we love you." Deeper into the pregnancy I wrote the news that he was a boy, that I'd been dealing with gestational diabetes, and that he seemed to love the Beatles, especially "In My Life."

When Henry was unnamed—"Dear You," a concept, a poppy seed—motherhood was a fantasy. And after Henry was born, for a time, the fantasy came to life.

May 30, 2013

Dear Henry,

You are waking up from a long nap right now, so I don't have much time to write. Wow, what a crazy couple of months. First of all, I love you even more than I expected, and I love love love staying home and hanging out with you all day—even though you scream your head off whenever we change your diaper, and you get fussy and cry for about an hour a day. But why am I starting with the negative? It's 7:20 p.m., and sunshine is streaming through our bedroom window and bathing you in lovely soft light, and you are squirming next to me on the bed, your little legs frogged out adorably. Your father and I will never get tired of staring at you. When one of us holds you, we will say to the other one—"look at this little cutie," or "check out this little monkey," or some variation. We are so in love with you.

Let me back up, to Thursday, April 18 at 8:30 p.m. I was home, sitting on the couch watching a movie (*Heartburn*) when your dad called me. His coworkers had just treated him to a daddy shower at an Irish pub, and he was calling from the subway, seeing if I wanted pizza or garlic knots. I told him what I had for dinner (canned salmon with tzatziki sauce on an English muffin and sautéed kale), and then I said, "Oh my god, my water is breaking." It felt and sounded like a balloon was popping in my body, which of course it was. I ran to the bathroom, where I was standing in a pool of water. Your dad kept saying, "Are you sure?" Yes, I was sure. This was it. You were on your way to us, exactly four weeks early. He rushed home and helped me pack for the hospital, luckily remembering your car seat down in the basement.

We got to Roosevelt Hospital around 10:15 p.m., and by the time they checked I was already 5 cm dilated—you were well on your way, and I was progressing fast. We were stuck between 9 and 10 cm for a while, and that was difficult. I wanted to push but wasn't allowed to, and that was a frustrating feeling. The contractions weren't as terrible as I thought they'd be. It helped to have your father there, and the midwife, Melissa, and an amazing nurse. It was a great support team, but the whole time it was really down to you and me. At our birth class the teacher suggested coming up with a mantra, and a couple of days prior I thought of one: "If he can do it, I can do it." And I kept thinking about that throughout the contractions, how crazy this must be for you, first to lose the water that had been your home and all you've known, and then to be pushed toward the outside world, ready or not. At 3 a.m. I started pushing, and that lasted a long time—four hours all told, which is two hours longer than normal. At a certain point the midwife was talking C section, and I just thought, I know I can push harder. The midwife who came on at 6 a.m., Susannah, brought out a mirror, and as soon as I actually saw your head (already covered in dark, soft hair), that was the motivation I needed—you slipped out about 30 minutes later, at 7:01 a.m. on Friday, April 19.

Right away the midwife put you on my chest, and I fell in love. We both did. Your father immediately broke down in racking sobs—which, as you likely know by now, is not usual for him. (It was the first of many times he broke down sobbing that week.) I reminded him to whisper your name in your ear, as your grandfather whispered the name "Jacob" into his ear. He sobbed his way through it, but he managed to whisper "Henry Felix Bergman" to you. What a beautiful name—and you were the first to hear it, aside from us two. I hope you like it as much as we do. Then we sang "Happy Birthday" to you—the first of many, I hope.

I remembered that moment so well. I remembered the euphoria of the day, and the months afterward, when my well of patience ran deep and when every day felt like a treasure. When I sang to Henry every night, "I love you more." I wished I could have held on to the gratitude I felt in those moments, and earlier, while I was pregnant and fantasizing about being a mother.

Now that motherhood was no longer a fantasy or a novelty, the reality was more complicated. You've heard the phrase "The days are long, but the years are short." If you're a parent, maybe you've said it yourself, because it rings so true. Why, though? Maybe because the days can be so grueling and our worst moments follow us after bedtime, into the laundry room with a stiff drink and a Joni Mitchell tearjerker.

But then, an hour or two later, we might peek into their bedrooms, comforted by the rise and fall of their chests. We might scroll through videos of them inventing knock-knock jokes. We are tired and beaten down, but we are still enthralled with these creatures we've created.

And those maddening moments? Those we don't write down. No Facebook pictures pop up to remind us of that time you yelled at your kid for throwing a bouncy ball near framed pictures. Our brains are kinder than we are, expunging those memories over time. That difficult day—as I write this a year later, I can't recall what made it so bad. And that failed thank you note to Henry? I went looking for it so I could quote verbatim, but it's lost. It's probably for the best. That amnesia is part of what makes the years seem short.

What we do remember as the years pass are the adorable faces our kids made—the way Charlie scrunched up his nose when he was puzzled, how Henry shook his shoulders as he ate a tasty meal. We remember the sweet and funny things our kids said because they turn into family jokes or because we capture them in videos or baby books.

The next day, before my second attempt to write thank you notes to my kids, I opened a note on my phone titled "Charlie and Henry Quotes" to remind myself of funny conversations I'd jotted down over the past few weeks.

- ♥ "Ugh you guys are so cute and I love you so much it almost makes me angry!!!" I said, and Henry replied, "Don't be angry, Mommy. Just be grateful we are here."
- ♥ Henry was trying out new words he knew. "Are you satisfied, Mommy? It means, do you have what you need?"

I did. Motherhood was no longer theoretical, but neither was my vast love for my children. Every parent learns that it's all temporary, every stage—the difficult ones and the adorable ones. As I write this, Charlie at three years old is driving us absolutely bananas—jumping from one tantrum to another, wailing when I leave the room to take a shower, biting his brother so hard he broke skin. It's okay to not be grateful for every minute, or every day, or every week.

My love for Henry and Charlie is what's permanent, and, as Nancy Tillman wrote in the book I've read thousands of times, it's "so high, so wide and so deep, it's always right there, even when you're asleep."

"Thank you for completing our family," I wrote to Charlie. "At one year, nine months you are an absolutely delightful and sweet little person who adores his big brother & whole family, and who picks up everything (counting to 10, building blocks) so well & so quickly. We all love you so much."

"Thank you," I wrote to Henry, "for making me a mommy five years ago. You changed my life. I'm so proud of the curious, creative, kind & compassionate little person you are. I'm honored to witness the transformation from little chicken to this complex & wonderful little boy. I love you."

That night at bedtime, Henry gave up his television show to help me put Charlie to bed. I sat between the two boys, nestling them into my body. Henry helped me sing "In My Life," our voices not quite harmonizing in the dark. He still remembered the words. Then we sang the Dido song I'd been singing to Charlie since the day we brought *him* home, when that round, dimpled face joined our family: "I want to thank you for giving me the best day of my life. And oh, just to be with you, is having the best day of my life."

HOW TO TEACH KIDS TO BE GRATEFUL

1. *Point out good things that are happening.* This could be a delicious food that you're eating, or a trip you're taking, or the house you're living in.

2. *Explain who is responsible for those things.* Often there are many people involved—from grandparents who saved up for the trip to the people who fly the airplane.

3. *Encourage your child to thank those people*—in a note or verbally. Help kids use specific language, identifying the ways in which the recipients helped and at what cost. Feelings are impactful here—how did this favor (or food or trip) make you feel?

4. *Model gratitude.* When you make gratitude a daily part of your life, you are showing your children how to think and act gratefully. Remember, your kids are like tiny, non-criminal stalkers: They are always watching.

CHAPTER FIVE

MAY: HEALTH

How Writing Notes to Healers
Can Help You Appreciate Life

LESSON: Thanking healers is therapeutic—for you and for them.

BENEFIT: Expressing gratitude boosts mental and physical health.

SURPRISE: A thank you habit leads to the most profound form of gratitude.

had an underlying reason for being grateful to be singing "In My Life" to baby Henry in our glider chair: There was a moment when I thought I wouldn't make it there. That letter I wrote to Henry about the day he was born, the one that ended with Jake and me singing "Happy Birthday" to him in the hospital room? The letter didn't end there. Here's what came next.

I don't want to talk too much about the next six days, but suffice it to say, Saturday night I came down with a 103 fever, and it turned out to be Strep A, which can get serious. I had to spend Monday night in the ICU, and there were nearly three days when I couldn't breastfeed you, and nearly two when I couldn't see you—that was a killer. Your father was at his wits' end—he needed to take care of me, but we both just wanted to hang out with you. Your grandmother was amazing through the week—she cancelled all her patients to be with us and help us. She brought lunch and snacks and various grooming products that I asked for. Without dwelling on it too much, I should say that there was a moment when I realized that things could get serious. You should know what I thought of in that moment. It was, first, that your father had given me thirteen happy years. I thought of our wedding and some of our big vacations, Paris and Bali, but I also thought of every night home alone with him—how much fun we have on the couch, him playing me music or us watching some show, always joking around and snuggling. The second thing I thought of was you. I made you, perfect you, and I was so proud of that. The Friday that we were cleared to go home, we were so relieved. The whole week I was just dreaming about taking you into your room and rocking you in our chair. And I finally got to do it.

When I saw the possibility of my own death, really saw it, and imagined its banal details—the gray clouds out the window might be the last thing I see; these scratchy sheets might be the last thing I feel—I finally understood its inevitability, and something cracked open inside me. I think the seed of this project was born out of that experience. I wanted to grip my life, and everyone in it, tightly and tenderly.

This May was an opportunity to look back at moments when a talented doctor or nurse or doula or physical therapist made a difference to my family, and to thank them. At the top of my list of healers, I wrote, "Went above and beyond."

Thanking Healers Is Therapeutic—for You and for Them

My first childbirth experience was, to say the least, traumatic. The nurses, though, were terrific. I sent them a thank you note and a basket of treats a week or two after I was released.

When I got pregnant for the second time, I started fresh with a new medical practice on the Upper East Side that gave me good vibes from the start. As I walked into the waiting room, the face that greeted me was my first boss's—illustrated and framed, hanging on the wall. Lisa Kogan had written about this team delivering her baby in her column for *O, The Oprah Magazine.* I walked over to read the article: "I'd like to take this moment to declare my undying love for these medical miracle workers." It felt like a good omen. Over the next few weeks, Jake and I met with two doctors in the practice—Michael Silverstein and Nathan Fox—who each answered our questions with empathy and patience.

It was a good thing I felt comfortable in that office, because I soon ran past the front desk and into the bathroom, doubled over in pain. Dr. Silverstein helped me through the next hours and made me feel less like a patient and more like a person going through a trauma. To him I wrote: "I am so grateful to you for your expertise and compassion on one of the most difficult days of my life. My miscarriage two years ago was intensely painful and bloody and awful—but you handled everything beautifully, and made me feel safe and relatively calm. (No small feat.) You're a terrific doctor and person."

Next, I turned to Dr. Fox, who delivered Charlie ten months later. After all my health scares and issues over the past four years—from infertility to gestational diabetes to potentially fatal infection to miscarriage—I was struck by how joyful his birth was. Oh, it was painful—but it produced the kind of pain that is assuaged by a miraculous procedure called an epidural, something I opted out of the first time around. To Dr. Fox I wrote: "I felt like I was in such capable, compassionate hands. Though this labor (my second) was incredibly painful, when I think back on it, what I remember most is my husband's love and your positive, joyful energy. You are so gifted at what you do."

He left me a voicemail thanking me, saying how nice the note was to read and that he hoped to be "around for many more wonderful events with you guys in the future." His tone was warm and delighted. I thought about his road to becoming a doctor—from the late-night studying to the grueling residencies to every early-morning emergency call. Money is not the motivator for that kind of dedication: There are easier ways to make a living. He and his colleagues and so many others put in that time so they can calmly and confidently guide us through the best and worst moments of our lives. Our vulnerable bodies are truly "in their hands," as I wrote, and when those hands are able and gentle, it makes all the difference.

When Henry was fourteen months old, he had surgery to remove his adenoids and insert ear tubes. Dr. Jay Dolitsky performed that surgery superbly and has since been a terrific ENT in every possible way. To him I wrote: "I've been reflecting lately on Henry's experience—from being stuffed up constantly with impaired hearing, to the thriving, healthy person he is now. From our first meeting we felt we were in great hands, and that has proven true, and then some. Thank you, also, for making Henry feel at ease."

In Dr. Dolitsky's reply voicemail, he expressed his "pleasure to be involved in Henry's care and watch him grow up as well."

The heartfelt thank you cards that seemed to mean something to these doctors each took me about four focused minutes to write. There's no statute of limitations, either. If anything, a delayed thank you note means *more*, because you are saying that you never forgot that person's role in a crucial time. As the years pass, your memories become more precious because they survived.

I will never forget my dad's two heart doctors, who saved his life ten years ago. To them I wrote: "I am so grateful to you for your care. That week started off really scary, but once we landed at Cedars Sinai and met with you, we breathed a collective sigh of relief. Thank you for taking such good care of my dad that week, and in the years since."

I thanked my dad's partner for her "presence of mind that day in Catalina. Your fast thinking & persistence saved Dad's life." And to my dad, I simply wrote: "As your Cedars Sinai anniversary approaches, I find myself reflecting on that week—one of the scariest (the scariest?) of my life. I am so grateful that you are around. I love you."

He left this voicemail: "Gina, I got your card today, actually last night. Thank you so much, honey. It's good to be with my children. It really is. Sometimes more than you know."

The note I wrote to my dad was all of three sentences—one of them three words long—scratched onto one side of a four-by-six lime green index card. It proved to be a simple, inexpensive form of therapy for both of us.

All told, I thanked a dozen health-care people. The remaining eighteen notes were addressed to a mix of neighbors (a helpful fishmonger, a dry cleaner who always remembers my name), friends (including Sharmaine, who was in from London and treated me to a fancy dinner), and parenting helpers (Henry's two exceptional pre-K teachers). I knew that the future would bring occasions that would necessitate thanking more health-care workers. But I couldn't have known then that in two years, during a global pandemic, thanking them would become a heartfelt nightly ritual for the entire city.

Expressing Gratitude Boosts Mental and Physical Health

While I was expressing gratitude for the people who've healed my dad, my son, and me, I felt that now-familiar sensation of my mind transitioning from frayed and frazzled to calm and focused, an almost meditative state. And that feeling carried into my day. Did it have a physiological underpinning? Was writing thank you notes providing me with real mental health benefits akin to meditation?

I asked Cory Allen, a meditation expert and the author of *Now Is the Way: An Unconventional Approach to Modern Mindfulness*.

"I would say that what you're feeling is *presence*," Allen said. "You set aside the distractions and mental fragmentations that come from living in the modern world. When you have the TV on while you're swiping through your phone while you're trying to eat dinner, that leaves the mind fragmented and unfocused, and ultimately it leaves you unrooted in your conscious experience. Your awareness begins to dim because of this pull in many different directions. One of the great benefits of meditation is creating and cultivating an amount of internal space. It gives you a sense of being aware of the arising thoughts and feelings that are coming into your mind and body.

"And so, in the process of writing those thank you notes," he continued, "you were tapping into a positive emotion, and you were narrowing down your focus. In addition, you were doing one thing repetitively, and that's sort of like a mantra. In meditation, the idea is that a mantra—repeating a phrase or even a sound—acts like a windshield wiper for the brain to keep it from becoming entangled in thoughts and narratives and stories. It's almost self-hypnotism. By repeating the same act of writing those cards over and over, it's acting like a physical mantra—which are very common in Buddhism. One example is when monks get together and make giant mandalas out of colored straws."

"Like rosaries," I pointed out, thinking of my (aptly named) great-aunt Rosie, who carried a rosary wherever she went. Allen agreed. By templating my thank you notes to make them easier to write, I had inadvertently created a mantra. This month, the batch to my dad's healers each started with "It's been nearly ten years since . . ." According to Allen, that simple windshield wiper of a phrase would clear my mind and allow the memories and more meaningful messages to flow.

I asked Allen how much of this mind-clearing benefit stemmed from the writing and how much from the gratitude. Would there be a similar effect if I sat with my grateful thoughts, or if I wrote a letter having nothing to do with gratitude? "I would say that to separate those things might not be a wise way to approach it," he said. "They are creating a sum greater than the parts. The writing is useful, and that can be meditative. The gratitude element can awaken the emotional embodiment of that feeling, which is also useful. By putting them together, you connect the emotional feeling and the intellectual feeling, and that creates the third thing.

"Do you know about the heart mind and the monkey mind?" he asked. I didn't, but he had my attention. "The monkey mind is a Buddhist term for the frantic, uncontrolled, chaotic, wandering mind. Your thoughts are buzzing all over the place, like a little monkey that's in a tree." I nodded furiously, wondering if he had sensed my monkey-buzzing mind by hearing my voice. "The heart mind means your intuitive, compassionate mind. It's thinking from a place of openhearted-ness, warmth, and connection to all living things.

"Having those two things working in harmony together is an aspiration through a meditation practice. In writing these notes, you accidentally stumbled into a way to connect the heart and monkey minds. You're bringing your emotions and your intellect into balance, and then through the repetitious nature of what you're doing, it puts you in that trancelike state of stillness.

"So, all of that combined, it is completely unsurprising to me that you would end up feeling more aware, less anxious, and more rooted in your gratitude and in your sense of embodiment of your experience."

He hit it, giving words to what I'd been feeling from those first train rides.

Gratitude itself improves health. According to studies by Robert A. Emmons and Michael McCullough, two of the world's premier positive psychology and gratitude experts, people who keep gratitude journals exercise more regularly, experience fewer symptoms of illness, and may recover from illnesses they do get more quickly. They also found that a person who experiences gratitude regularly gets more hours of sleep.

By writing these cards and establishing an active gratitude habit—which I was starting to realize I would carry with me beyond this one year—I was connecting my heart and monkey minds in a meditative way, and improving my health in the process.

A Thank You Habit Leads to the Most Profound Form of Gratitude

I've thought a lot about death during this project, morbid as it might sound. For me, writing an openhearted thank you note to someone is a reminder of mortality—mine and theirs.

Before sliding a card in the mailbox, I've sometimes imagined someone decades down the line, long after I am gone, finding that card, now tattered, in a box or between the pages of a book. What would they learn of me? Of the recipient? What traits would come through? What sentiments would remain? Is there something in there that's interesting, or original, or just honest and kind?

We hang on to birthday or holiday cards from deceased relatives because these tokens are what's left and can shed light on who they were. A typewritten card from my paternal grandmother, Beverly, includes the recipe for pierogi that she learned to make for my grandfather, who loved those Eastern-European-by-way-of-Ohio dishes. She was dedicated to him, and it gave her joy to feed him well. She was also a social butterfly, reflected in this update: "My birthday party was a success. Had 35 guests . . . among them a judge, two doctors, and so many friends and relatives."

As the neurologist and author Oliver Sacks approached death, he sat down to write his final thoughts, collected in a book of essays called *Gratitude*. "I cannot pretend I am without fear," he wrote. "But my predominant feeling is one of gratitude. . . . I have had an intercourse with the world, the special intercourse of writers and readers. Above all, I have been a sentient being, a thinking animal, on this beautiful planet, and that in itself has been an enormous privilege and adventure."

Now that he's gone, his beautiful words remain. It's the most primitive motivator for making art: To be remembered is to live on. Correspondence is like that, on a smaller scale. I started to wonder if this humble genre was even more important than the great American novel. What if a thank you card has more staying power, in its limited circle, than a bestseller? Books go out of print, or they get tossed. So, too, do many cards. But the memorable ones, those that speak a heartfelt truth, however tiny—they might be waiting in a memory box for future generations to discover.

Deathbed regrets are mostly stuff you didn't do or didn't say. This project has been my way of saying *everything*. I'm leaving a paper trail.

And while a thank you has no statute of limitations, there is not unlimited time. I hadn't seen my friend John in three or four years but had been thinking of him and planned to write to him in July, during my food month. But he died in April.

I met John and his wife, Marie, when I was working as an editorial assistant at *O*. I had set my sights on working at a food magazine—my dream job was travel editor at *Food & Wine*—and so I signed up for an Italian wine class, figuring that I would learn the difference between a Barolo and a Barbaresco and make some like-minded friends in the process. I hadn't imagined those friends would be a sixty-something couple from New Jersey.

John was generally the tallest man in the room, and always the most generous. He once told me that when he was a kid he wanted to be Santa Claus when he grew up. It gave him such pleasure—once his four daughters were grown, and he had made good money as an actuary—to drive into Manhattan and treat friends to a luxurious meal. That was how I, at twenty-three, ended up dining at some of the city's swankiest restaurants. John was also an incredible listener. I always left our dinners feeling not only well fed but well tended to.

It was too late to write to John, so I wrote to his widow. "I've been thinking so much about you and John, and how it was my lucky day when we were seated at the same table at Becco. I treasure the memories of our fabulous, fancy dinners. What an incredibly special treat for a twenty-something food lover with very little disposable income. I remember particularly fun dinners at Babbo, Little Giant, & Daniel— that was the first time a waiter gave my bag its own little stool, ha. I loved that John always ordered pink Champagne to start the meal. What a perfectly festive & joyful tradition—one I've kept up. I'm so grateful to you both for including me in those lavish dinners—and for your friendship. I miss John, and I am sending you a lot of love & gratitude."

A couple of months later, Marie reached out: "I meant to write to you before to tell you how much I loved (and how much it meant to me . . . and my family when I shared it with them) the thank you note you sent me. The way you spoke about the very first time we met and what it meant to you . . . that made me smile, cry, reminisce—all at the same time!! It was such a delight—and joy to my soul—to receive that note from you."

Condolence cards function similarly to thank you notes, I realized. Ideally, they shed light on the deceased by sharing a specific memory. It's a final thank you to the person who is gone, addressed to their loved ones.

"A eulogy is, above all, the simple and elegant search for small truths," Tom Chiarella wrote in an article in *Esquire* called "How to Give a Eulogy." His advice works for a sympathy card, too, and for a meaningful thank you note.

The year after John died was even harder for Marie than those first raw months. She wrote to me, wanting to know if I had any practical advice on how she could go on her own gratitude journey. "Did you take your Rolodex and start from A, continuing to Z, or did you follow a calendar system—when did this person come into my life? I really want to do this because your note made such an impact. It truly touched me!"

I passed along my advice and tips, a sort of CliffsNotes version of this book, and offered to be her tutor. It won't be difficult for her to identify those "small truths" about John. Perhaps writing them down and sharing them with the people who loved him, and thanking them for sharing in that love, will help her process her grief.

And then those notes will be out in the world, waiting to be found by a future reader, who might be inspired to treat a friend to a fancy dinner, starting with pink Champagne.

HOW TO IDENTIFY AND THANK HEALERS

1. *Recall pivotal health moments.* Start by thinking about your body and what it's been through. Then consider those moments for your family members.

2. *Identify the health providers who went above and beyond.* These could be doctors, nurses, doulas, shrinks, or physical therapists who were exceptionally good at their job or who treated you like a person instead of just a patient.

3. *Remember the people who helped you emotionally.* Extra-supportive family members and friends can also be healers.

4. *Create a template for the first sentence.* If you're writing a batch of notes about one health crisis, start each one the same way. This not only makes your job easier but also acts as a meditative mantra, clearing out your mind and helping you focus on specific memories.

5. *Write from the heart.* Describe what you remember about that person's role in your crisis—something specific that they said or did while you were in their care and how that made you feel.

CHAPTER SIX

JUNE: HOME

What Skipping the Notes Can Teach You

SURPRISE: Embracing imperfection is key to accomplishing your goals.

LESSON: Social feeds are a poor substitute for connection.

BENEFIT: Identifying grateful feelings gets easier with practice.

At this point, I was feeling pretty confident. Nearly halfway through my year of expressing gratitude, I had found my rhythm and was starting to feel like I might actually accomplish the ambitious goal I'd set for myself.

But there was a hiccup: I had recently wrapped up my consultancy at Boll & Branch, which meant no more quiet hours on New Jersey Transit. Instead, I walked thirty minutes along the Brooklyn waterfront to a co-working space in Dumbo that I'd joined earlier in the year. I was spending most of my office hours pitching potential new clients and writing branded content, about windows or jarred salad dressing or French-inspired yogurt. My final health-related thank you notes had provided a welcome break from copywriting, and I was excited to start on my June batch of cards. Parenting and health had been big, serious topics. Home would be lighter, more fun.

What do I love most about my home? I asked myself as a first prompt while sitting at a table overlooking the Brooklyn Bridge. I closed my eyes and answered: "The people in it." I rolled my eyes, annoyed at my own earnestness. I had already written to Jake, Henry, and Charlie, and I had my family month waiting for me.

I tried another: *What would I miss most if I moved?* Easy, our Mews neighbors. Our house has an odd, wonderful setup. Walk out the front door, past our grill and smoker, and you'll see a gate to the adjoining building's bike area. Walk through that and you'll reach the Mews—a row of four little townhouses, each containing two kids. On weekends we keep our doors open and the kids run freely back and forth, borrowing one another's bikes and soccer balls. We have a potluck grill cookout a couple of times a year. We have a running group text where we ask each other for spare keys and WD-40 and offer homemade cookies and marshmallows. It's the best.

But I had already written to some of these friends in my neighbors month.

How about this: *Who has improved my house or something in it?* Oh yes! I had one! I pulled out a note card. "Dear Richard," I wrote. "Thank you for your terrific work fixing our Internet. You went above & beyond. I truly never thought I'd write a thank you note to an employee of a cable company—but you were 100% on top of our issues from the get go. And in fixing our Internet issues you made our home safer, and alerted us to water damage (which we are working to fix). Thank you also for crediting us for the broken pot in such a timely fashion. You're a gem!"

Richard really was a gem, and I was glad to tell him so.

There was also Tomas, a handyman who had completed projects around our old apartment as we were getting ready to put it on the market. He'd then helped us when we were settling into our new place: installing a light fixture, repainting a windowsill. But I'd already written him a thank you note in March, after calling to see if he was free to repaint a bedroom, and he broke the news that he was about to retire—and move to Colombia. I'd wasted no time writing and mailing this thank you note: "It's so clear how much pride you take in your work. You were always such a pleasant person to have around, too. We will miss you! (Especially your "best friend" Henry!)"

Then there was our housekeeper, Angela, who has dusted, mopped, and swept our home every week or two for more than a decade, and who brings us packages of jerk-spiced fish, and whom our kids adore. (I acknowledge my privilege here. Working Angela into our budget has brought us immeasurable joy and prevented countless marital squabbles, and I would sooner give up vacations and restaurants than give up her incredible services.) I had already written Angela a thank you note, an off-topic card, in April: "Thank you for being so helpful and supportive on that scary carbon monoxide day—and for being helpful always. Thank you also for the delicious fish, which we love. You're the best and we are so grateful!"

I had been driving to New Jersey when Angela called, sounding upset yet calm as she said, "There's a fire truck at your house, and they want to come inside." Turns out, our carbon monoxide detector had gone off, alerting the fire department, and firefighters were about to break down our door when Angela arrived. She was indispensable that whole day, even driving to pick up Henry from school while Jake dealt with various authorities. The carbon monoxide leak could have been deadly, but thanks to our alarm system and the help of many people, including Angela, everyone was safe.

That was what really mattered when it came to your home, right?

Embracing Imperfection Is Key to Accomplishing Your Goals

To summarize: Of my three home improvers who weren't family members or neighbors, I'd previously written thank yous to two of them.

But I wanted to solve this problem, so I tried one more prompt. *What else about my house do I love?* The built-in bookshelves. The black-and-white ocean waves wallpaper in the kids' room. I gamely considered researching the shelf carpenter and the wallpaper designers. Instead, I decided to do the scary thing and bail on this month.

It's what I would have done had I been an editor in chief faced with a magazine theme that wasn't working. At *O*, every issue had a unifying theme—mothers, jealousy, passion, aging. Once in a while, the top editors scrapped a theme if they felt the proposed story ideas weren't strong enough.

If I kept tinkering with this puzzle, grasping for a batch of home-related thank you notes that inspired me, the whole project would languish. One month behind would become two, then three, and before long I would be the woman who wrote 152 thank you notes in six months, which didn't have quite the same ring to it.

More than a year later, with my 365 notes long completed, I find myself *still* trying to solve the problem. I jotted down this too-late, why-are-you-even-trying prompt: *Find the 30 objects in your house that you love most, and thank either their maker or their giver. Examples: Mom's old charm bracelet. The vanity that Brigitte spotted in Greenpoint. The poster Jake brought home from the Louisiana Museum.*

And listen, if you are intrigued by the idea of a home month, that would be one way to accomplish it. The stuff you love most is still just stuff, and it needs a person and a story behind it to make for a worthwhile thank you note.

Or, if you're a person with good taste who designed your house, you might have a whole list of contractors and artisans to thank and OH MY GOD I'M STILL DOING IT!

It (obviously) went against my dogged nature to quit, but this project had already taught me to embrace imperfection. Writing 365 meaningful notes in a year is a tall order no matter what stage of life you're in. But right then, with two little kids and a hustle-or-die career, I was only able to forge on by rejecting every time- or money-sucking obstacle that arose.

Should I splurge on the nice note cards? While I love thick, letter-press cards, those $5 price tags add up fast. After the first, sticker-shocking month, I bought a set of one hundred colorful, functional note cards and envelopes at Target.

Should I outline these notes before writing them? Nope. An extra step takes time I don't have. If I make a mistake, I cross it out. If I go on a tangent, I find a way to meander back to the point.

Should I write as neatly as possible? Maybe, but I don't. I write as fast as my thoughts come and try my best to keep it legible.

Should I worry about expressing everything this person means to me? No, I keep these notes short and to the point. (It's best if there's a specific point.)

Should I try to make each note as poetic as possible? No need for literary preening. Better to focus on the recipient and speak from the heart.

One of my biggest obstacles had been the constantly looming deadlines. The deadlines and my advance planning helped me stay on track, but I was always a week or two (or more) behind in *drafting* the notes. Addressing and mailing them might take another few weeks. I combated any guilty feelings by reminding myself that these deadlines were self-imposed and entirely made up. To move forward, I had to get comfortable lagging behind.

That my home month turned out to be a dud was just one more obstacle I had to knock over. Quitting, however, meant that I was sticking myself with an extra batch of notes—topic TBD—to complete before the end of the year in order to accomplish my 365-card goal. A worry for another time.

Social Feeds Are a Poor Substitute for Connection

In the weeks it took me to come to this decision, I was walking around without a stack of cards to turn to in my downtime. Like a relapsed addict, I started picking up my phone more. In the beginning of the year, I had found myself slack-jawed and scrolling on New Jersey Transit as if in a stupor. This time, I had a keen awareness of the habit and the way it was making me feel: frayed, disconnected, scattered. And yet, even being mindful of this, I found it hard to stop.

I knew I wasn't alone. Social media causes a similar reaction in the brain to recreational drugs, I'd heard. Casino slots are a more accurate comparison, according to the neuroscientists who study social media's effects on the brain.

When you get a social media notification, your brain sends a feel-good chemical messenger called dopamine along one of your brain's reward pathways. Dopamine is also triggered by exercise, sex, delicious food, drugs, love, and—here's the relevant one—positive social interactions, like laughing faces, recognition by peers, and messages from loved ones.

Those brain pathways get the tingles even in anticipation of their dopamine hit. When the hit actually happens—when a chubby-faced baby picture in your feed triggers a reward—the association strengthens the frequently used connections between neurons by increasing the intensity of the response. Your brain likes the feeling; it feels better and better; it craves more. And there it is—addiction.

Even worse, our brains have this glitch called "reward prediction error encoding," which basically means your brain gets hooked on dopamine rewards more readily when they're delivered at random. It's something casino owners know all too well. When playing slots, there's intense anticipation while those wheels are turning: The moments between the lever pull and the outcome provide time for our dopamine neurons to increase their activity. The game itself creates a rewarding feeling.

If we think a reward is going to be delivered at random, and if checking for the reward comes at little cost, we end up checking habitually. Social feeds once updated chronologically. Then the algorithms changed to implement a random reward pattern similar to casino slots—that's by design. You are incentivized to spend more time on your feeds. And the brain rewires itself, wanting more likes and comments, more smiling faces and mildly interesting news. Too much social media is altering our actual brain chemistry. Basically, we are all sitting in our homes staring at miniature slot machines with an unlimited supply of social stimuli that act as tiny dopamine hits, and it's no wonder we find it hard to step away.

Chamath Palihapitiya, the former vice president of user growth at Facebook, was speaking at the Stanford business school on the topic of "money as an instrument of social change" when a student asked about his role in exploiting consumer behavior. "I feel tremendous guilt," he responded. "The short-term, dopamine-driven feedback loops that we have created are destroying how society works."

Not to put too fine a point on it.

And listen, slots can be fun! Who doesn't love that gambling thrill? Who doesn't like a picture of a floppy-eared puppy? I'm not suggesting that we delete our apps. These hits of dopamine were a lifeline when we were stuck in our homes during the Covid-19 shutdown. And sometimes they were much more. They were dazzling dance performances, uproarious comedy routines—every day our phones brought us great art and a sense of solidarity. But as with anything else dopamine-related, I want to be mindful of the slippery slope toward digital addiction. I want to approach the slots with $20 in coins, and when that bucket is empty, I want to *step away*.

While reading up on how the brain rewires itself to crave more smiling faces and thumbs-up likes and flattering comments, I thought back to my conversation with Cory Allen, the meditation expert. He'd explained how positive thinking can also have a powerful influence in rewiring our brains.

"Cultivating warmth and love in the heart can be an active practice," he said. "You can actually sit in your meditation and think of your child and the warmth that comes with that. Being able to sit with that feeling is remarkably transformative to your emotional state because of the shift of neuroplasticity through common brain states. Plastic means it's moldable, shapeable."

Bret Stetka, author of *A History of the Human Brain*, confirmed that "sitting with any feeling, whether positive, neutral or negative, has the potential to rewire our neural connections due to our neuro-plastic brains. Specifically, feelings of love and warmth are conjured through the interconnections involved in the 'reward' regions of your brain, such as amygdala, prefrontal cortex, and striatum, all working together with oxytocin—aka the 'cuddle hormone'—from the hypo-thalamus."

Stetka explained further: "Thoughts send nerve signals traveling down axons, which are long cellular extensions that make contact with shorter extensions on neighboring neurons called dendrites. Where the axon meets the dendrite is the synapse, where the neu-rotransmitters release." That's how thinking works. And because our brains evolved to be as efficient as possible, whenever we think in habitual ways, those pathways that the nerve signals are com-municating along will start to rewire so that it's less taxing on the brain.

Allen had given this example: "Math might seem abstract and challenging. But if you take a hard-core math class for one hour per day, all of a sudden you'll be able to do math easily. That same concept applies to our emotional states—in our optimism and in the way we see the world. These things remap and change based on how we are thinking. So doing something like connecting your focus and sitting with a feeling of positivity, or thinking of a child, if you make that a part of your practice, you will begin to retrain the way that you hold and build emotional responses into your day. You can alter the way you see the world."

Social feeds can rewire the brain, but so, too, could my thank you notes. They'd been acting as little warriors, battling my run-of-the-modern-day-mill smartphone addiction.

Social media is where many of us spend the majority of our free time, if we're honest. And our collective hobby largely comes down to either admiring what other people have (Instagram) or going down a rage spiral (Facebook, Twitter). Expressing gratitude in the form of a thank you note has been the perfect antidote: time spent on something purely positive, honoring the things, people, memories that are mine.

We reach for our phones because we crave companionship. But social media, while fun, is ultimately a poor substitute. If we can be mindful of the actual thing we are craving, and if we can swap out some of that scroll time for real connection, we're rewarded with a feeling of contentment and peace, that sensation I first felt on the train back in January. Connection could take the shape of writing to friends or calling Mom or talking to strangers or even sitting still with ourselves. Our own thoughts can be very good company if we let them.

Identifying Grateful Feelings Gets Easier with Practice

Toward the end of June, once I put down my phone—or tried to; it's a process—and gave up on the home theme, I noticed something. I was starting to express thanks in real time, in a more verbal way than I ever had before—evidence, perhaps, of my newly rewired, more grateful brain.

One hectic morning I was in a subway station, running late for a meeting uptown, when I realized I'd forgotten my wallet and, therefore, my ability to take the subway. I summoned a Lyft with my phone—which, thankfully, I had remembered. The driver, Chiou, sensed my anxiety and spent the whole ride readjusting his route, checking and rechecking. During those thirty minutes I would have normally spent panicking in traffic, I focused on how Chiou was trying to help me. As we crossed through Central Park, it became clear that his method had paid off: He'd shaved seven minutes off our estimated commute and would get me there just in time. I thanked him and told him about my morning—about the forgotten wallet and the important meeting. I told him that he was good at his job. I tipped him well, but our stories are another form of currency, and they're free. "Good luck today!" he shouted after me.

Realizing I would also have to splurge on a pricey car home, I texted my in-laws, who live nearby. While I worked, Lu left a $20 bill with her doormen, Sam and Angel, both of whom greeted me with hugs when I picked up the cash.

My gratitude for all the people who helped me that morning colored the rest of the day, which, I noticed, was lovely and sunny. When I got home to relieve Rhonda, our nanny, I saw how neat the house looked and texted her to say thank you. As I sat down at my desk, I admired (for the thousandth time) my friend Chloe's beautiful painting of flowers. Instead of letting the thought pass unremarked upon, I texted Chloe a picture and told her how much they brightened the space.

We all have these fleeting feelings of happiness and gratitude, and there is a simple way to extend them: We can share them with the people responsible. That was what I was training myself to do. When a grateful thought or compliment entered my mind, I was learning to take note of it, then act on it.

The world is full of small things to be grateful for. We all know this, but recognizing those things takes practice. For going on a decade, Jimmy Fallon has been reading thank you notes on his shows—*The*

Tonight Show, and *Late Night* before it: "Thank you, quilts, for being blankets made of other tiny blankets"; "Thank you, website button that says 'Forgot My Password,' for basically being my password."

I spoke to the writer Jeremy Bronson, who created this running gag a decade ago. He was trying to think of a recurring bit for Jimmy when he spotted a new Diet Coke flavor in a grocery store. "I looked at it," he said, "and thought, you could thank this Diet Coke for existing and make that funny."

How had viewing the world with this thank you note lens affected him? I wondered. "I would walk around and be a little more mindful, a little bit more aware of something that needed to be called out, or something that demanded a little bit of gratitude," he said. "When as part of your job you are expected to write a bunch of gratitude notes every week, I wouldn't be surprised if it made all of us slightly more aware of who we should give thanks to."

When you're looking for things to be grateful for, you'll start seeing them everywhere. Some might seem trivial to the point of absurd—like a new diet soda flavor—but those tiny things provide miniature rushes that add up to a grateful frame of mind.

HOW TO RECOGNIZE AND EXPRESS GRATITUDE IN THE MOMENT

1. ***Catch your grateful thought.*** As quick, fleeting moments of gratitude arise, hold on to them. *This customer service rep is actually being helpful*, you might (someday) think. (I told you I was an optimist.) Or, *Last night's dinner party was so nice.*

2. ***Express your gratitude on the spot, adding your feelings and a compliment.*** To the rep, on the call: "Thank you for taking the time to advocate for me. I was dreading this call, but I'm relieved that you picked up the phone. You are really good at your job." To the host, via text or phone call: "What a terrific party full of lovely people and food. I felt so comfortable in your home. You made it all look so easy."

3. ***Follow up.*** Writing an online review or calling a manager can give the gesture more impact.

4. ***Take notes.*** Jot down these moments of active gratitude and watch how they add up with practice.

5. ***Go out on a limb.*** If there's a shy inner voice stopping you from fully expressing your gratitude, try to quash it. The awkwardness you perceive lives only in your head—it's science (see page 98 in chapter 7).

CHAPTER SEVEN

JULY: FOOD

How Writing Notes to People Who've Enhanced Your Life Can Enhance Theirs

BENEFIT: Expressing gratitude leads to generosity.

SURPRISE: A lot of people are going through something a lot of the time.

LESSON: Any squirminess you might feel is unfounded.

I had an incentive to ditch my floundering home month: I couldn't wait to get cracking on the next topic.

When I'd brainstormed themes for my Thank You Year back in January, neighbors, family, friends, and mentors were the first, obvious choices. Then, something incongruous came to mind: food! I didn't think through how this month might play out, practically speaking. Would I thank cookbook authors? Food writers? Chefs, farmers, dinner party hosts? But in that moment the entire project seemed to click into place, and I knew the year was going to be not only gratifying but fun. I felt entirely comfortable writing about food: It was something I used to do for a living.

I remember when I first heard the word "foodie" in the early aughts. *This is an unfortunate word*, I thought, *but at least there's a name for what I am.* When I was twenty-two, I devoured *Gourmet* editor in chief

Ruth Reichl's latest memoir while dog-sitting at my colleague Val's very grown-up-seeming apartment. That night I took myself out to dinner at BCD Tofu House, a Koreatown restaurant that Reichl wrote about in the book. While finishing my perfect square of custard-like tofu, I decided that I wanted to be a food writer. I announced the goal at a party in Murray Hill shortly thereafter. "Like, a restaurant critic?" someone responded. This was in 2002, when the Food Network was less than a decade old and food writing was not a high-profile career path.

Nevertheless, I became an editor at food magazines, first at *Rachael Ray Every Day*, where the word "foodie" was on our banned list, then at *Food & Wine*, where the term was allowed but only sparingly. Food was also my hobby. I would dedicate weekends to finding the best soup dumplings or throwing elaborate dinner parties (one theme: Baruch a Thai, a Jewish-Thai mash-up).

In short, food is a huge part of my identity. I recently sent my friend Jorma a condolence note after his grandmother died, and he wrote back, "She really loved life and lived it." I responded, "I would love that to be my epitaph." He replied, without skipping a beat, "Yours should have a food mention, I think?"

While friends still think of me as a food person, I often wonder—*beep!* need to flip over the fish sticks—if it's still true. At home I'm mostly a fry cook, throwing together/defrosting quick meals. Ask me for a restaurant recommendation, and you'll receive one within walking distance of my home. (Granted, my Brooklyn neighborhood has a Beyoncé-approved pizza joint, three or four world-class cocktail bars, and a Thai place so spicy you'll leave sweating.) As for work, food writing, a casualty of Instagram and the collapse of magazines, is no longer my main gig.

In recent months, as I write this chapter, mild health issues have led to my giving up refined sugar, gluten, and dairy. Dairy! You might remember that I wrote a note to Gianluca from our beloved "mozz-a-YA-YA store" in our neighborhood. Indeed, I once wrote an essay about my love for mozzarella in a cheese magazine called *Culture*. ("While it may not be the world's most interesting or multilayered cheese, it's dairy distilled down to its cleanest, most perfect form.") *I wrote a cookbook about nachos.* Now I have eggs and kimchi for breakfast and snack on walnuts and tins of smoked mussels and have basically become an accidental ascetic.

While writing my list of July recipients, I wondered: Would thanking the people responsible for memorable restaurant meals and dinner parties and my food-entrenched career reconnect me to my former foodie self?

Expressing Gratitude Leads to Generosity

One of my thank you note rules: no outlining beforehand. It's a fussy extra step that just slows you down. So, I started to write to Ruth Reichl the same as always—with a pen and card and no clear plan in mind. "Dear Ms. Reichl, Reading your memoir *Tender at the Bone* influenced the course . . ." Then I stopped. Can you "influence" a course? I tossed that card and tried again. "Dear Ms. Reichl, I didn't know what I wanted to be until I read . . ." I didn't like that, either.

And so, for the first time that year, I broke my rule and typed out the letter to my idol in a Word doc before transferring the crafted message onto a pretty card—an upgrade from my trusty Target note card. At the mailbox, I had to quash the inner voice that imagined her scoffing at this letter. Nevertheless, I sent it. "Reading *Tender at the Bone* changed the course of my career. It made me realize that food writing was something a person can do, and if that were true, I wanted to do it. I started saying it out loud. Then my mentor Frank

Lalli, whom I knew from interning at *George* magazine, recruited me to help launch Rachael Ray's magazine. I was still working there when *Gourmet* folded. I felt physically sick. How could I realize my dream of someday working at *Gourmet* if there was no *Gourmet*? Also, what would I cook? To this day I trust *Gourmet* recipes more than any others. (Don't tell Dana or Tina from *F&W*, ha. I went on to become their travel editor.) I make the jook with chicken and ginger for my husband's birthday every year, and the pea soup with pumpernickel croutons for my son's half birthday.

"I loved reading your latest book. I was laid off from *F&W*, so I could relate on many levels. Thank you for writing such beautiful books, and for making such a perfect magazine. I don't know where my background in food journalism will take me, the media landscape being what it is. But I'm incredibly grateful for the skills I developed and the people I met. People who love food truly are the best people."

I was paraphrasing Julia Child: "People who love to eat are always the best people." Take Diana Sturgis, who co-directed the test kitchen at *Rachael Ray Every Day*. One day I stopped by the kitchen and sampled perfect hot cross buns right out of the oven. Heaven. The next day Diana handed me the recipe, handwritten, and it's now tucked into my recipe binder. "It's so indicative of your generosity and sweetness," I wrote to her. And she replied, in a card I got in the mail a few weeks later: "The recipe is one that I taught to my high school students in Wales over 50 years ago! Now I really want one, but eat 'gluten-free,' so forget it." Diana's co-director, Tracey Seaman, and her team baked me a cake every year on my birthday. At their core, food people are generous.

I was lucky to work with some of the world's best food brains, including *Food & Wine*'s former food director, the legendary Tina

Ujlaki. "I've been thinking about my three years at *F&W* and what a privilege it was to join the ranks of the food elite," I wrote to her. "Thank you for always being generous with your time and your incredible food knowledge. I loved my glimpses into the test kitchen; I loved brainstorming in the meetings. One highlight was our dessert tasting at Paul Liebrandt's place in Tribeca. I'm remembering an unbelievable concord grape and black sesame composed dessert. What a fun night—what a fun few years."

I brought home so many wonderful recipes and techniques from work that for a period of time there, my kitchen was turning out some truly delicious food. But when I became a mother, I lost my mojo. One cookbook helped me get it back, so I wrote to the author, Jenny Rosenstrach. "Dear Jenny," I started. "I'm using your first name because I feel like I know you. I was struggling to get back into the kitchen and find joy there when I found *Dinner: The Playbook*. I needed a way to transition from my previous life as a proficient, eager cook, always trying out new recipes, to my new life with an infant. For months, I fed the baby and my husband fed me. Which I love/loved . . . but I missed cooking. Your book gave me back my confidence, and laid out a little plan for me in the kitchen. At this point I've made nearly all the recipes—the book is truly battered & splattered. Chicken parm meatballs are on heavy rotation, as is the chorizo frittata. I actually love to cook . . . thank you for helping me remember that!"

The people who most influence our day-to-day meals are the ones who run our favorite farmer's market stand, Lani's. "Dear Nermin," I wrote. "Visiting Lani's is a highlight of the week for us—not only because of your gorgeous vegetables (which we plan our entire weekly menu around) but because you are so kind and friendly to me and Jake and our kids, Henry and Charlie. Thank you for everything you do!"

That two-sentence thank you note has had a big impact. Henry delivered it to Nermin—I'd jotted down the spelling of his name the week before—and we all started calling him by name. He, in turn, started greeting all of *us* by name. Every week, to this day, he saves us two cartons of eggs and gifts the boys with giant muffins—zucchini for Henry, pumpkin for Charlie. It started making me uncomfortable: Getting free stuff was never the motivation for this project. I shopped by myself one week, and when Nermin pressed the muffins into my hand, I told him there was no need, that he'd already been so generous. He insisted. Giving my kids these treats made Nermin feel good, I realized. It was okay to accept the gift. This Christmas, we delivered Nermin a batch of chocolate chip cookies, and he showed us a picture of himself at the farm stand the week he started managing it, twenty-one years prior. As we were leaving, Henry turned to me and said, "Nermin is the sweetest farmer in the world."

The last note recipients on my list worked in our favorite restaurants. Thanking them was more emotional than I'd expected.

When I moved to New York at age twenty-one, seeking out the best (mostly very cheap) restaurants became the way I explored the city. And then restaurants became more than that—they were homes away from home, defining each era in my life. In my mid-twenties it was Little Giant on the Lower East Side, and after we moved to Brooklyn it was Prime Meats, Battersby, and Pok Pok. As I sat down to thank staffs, I realized how important these restaurants had been at each stage, and not so much because of the food.

I wrote to Jen, the former host at Prime Meats. "I've been thinking about our early experiences at Prime Meats, which we loved so much, and realizing that so much of what we loved about the place was because of you. You really created that warmth and genuinely great hospitality that made us feel so at home."

And I wrote to Erika, who used to run the front of house at Battersby. "Before the entire city/world discovered it, it was our little place, and it felt like stepping into a little bit of magic in our neighborhood. The food was/is incredible, yes—but so much of that magic was because of you. Have you ever heard that quote, not sure whose it is (Danny Meyer?)—'You go to a restaurant for the food; you come back for the service.' Our Battersby experience showed me how true that is. Thank you for being so good at your job; for always making us feel SO welcome; for saving us spots at the bar—and for being you. The restaurant isn't at all the same without you!"

Our most recent hangout, the extra spicy Thai place Pok Pok, around the corner from our home, was where we ate the night I learned I was pregnant with Henry. One summer day, after writing a batch of notes, I walked by the restaurant and saw a letter in the window from the chef, Andy Ricker; he was announcing that he would close up shop in September. To him, I wrote: "I had one blessed night alone in the city without my family, and I was thrilled to spend it at the bar at Pok Pok, with a pineapple cocktail and catfish. To say we will miss Pok Pok is such a wild understatement. But thank you for these spicy-wonderful years; thank you for introducing us to laab and jasmine rice water and khao soi and durian custard (my pregnancy craving) and spicy peanuts and too many wings and all the rest. Thank you, also, for writing such a thoughtful goodbye letter. It does heal some of the sting."

Cheeky's in Palm Springs provided something different but also important: an absolutely perfect breakfast—especially their thin, crisp-chewy waffles topped with salted butter. Over the years I'd become friendly with the chef, Tara Lazar, and to her I wrote: "I can't tell you how often I think of Cheeky's waffles, bacon sampler platter, and Bloody Mary. Thank you for being so generous with your recommendations and favors (you've saved a table for many a friend over the years)."

Tara emailed to tell me she'd be in Brooklyn the following week. I invited her over for pea soup with pumpernickel croutons (the *Gourmet* recipe, of course). While laughing at something Jake said, I remember leaning back and thinking how special it was to cook for one of the food people I'd identified this month, all of whom had been so generous and provided me with so much pleasure.

"Thank you for the waffles!"

home-cooked dinner

surprise gift

As Tara was leaving, I complimented her Adidas sneakers, which were embroidered with royal blue and teal leaves. The following week, *she sent me those sneakers in my size.* I would have thought that, unlike Tara, I was not cool enough to pull them off. But, as I wrote to her in a follow-up thank you note, "OK these shoes are actually my favorites! I've worn them like one-third to one-half of the days since they arrived. So comfy, fun, chic—PERFECT for Brooklyn working mom life. This was such a special, unexpected present & I love it. So glad we're in touch. Hope to see you in PS or NYC soon. Meantime, say hello to your waffles for me!"

Generosity leads to gratitude, which leads to generosity.

A Lot of People Are Going Through Something a Lot of the Time

You never forget your first love, and for me and Jake that was Little Giant. The summer of 2005 is immortalized in my memory. I'd just left my first job out of college (*O, The Oprah Magazine*) and was thrilled to no longer be an assistant. At twenty-five, I was a full-fledged editor, at a food publication, no less: I was launching Rachael Ray's magazine with a small but stellar staff of people who became lifelong friends, including Sara—whom I reconnected with this year—and Nick Fauchald. One afternoon, when I was trying to decide where to meet friends for dinner, Nick showed me the menu for Little Giant, full of summery-sounding foods (wax beans, pickled watermelon rinds). We went, and I immediately felt at home. The space was tiny but not cramped, thanks to the breezy, wide-open windows looking onto the vibrant corner of Orchard and Broome on the Lower East Side. Each plate of deviled eggs, chicken liver mousse, buttermilk-chive biscuits, and sticky toffee pudding looked like a still life in the natural light pouring through the windows, and then in the warm candlelight as the sun went down. No dish lasted for more than a few minutes: We were practically fighting over the crumbs. The vibe was happy and social, which fit my mood.

Jake and I spent the summer becoming restaurant regulars for the first time, even though it took the better part of an hour to travel home to the Upper West Side. We hosted so many friends there. The picture I had turned into a postcard for my friend Megan, on which I wrote that we'd looked like "American Apparel models"—that was taken at Little Giant. I invited Marie and John (the man who started meals with pink Champagne) and attempted to pick up the tab for once. (Fat chance.) Jake and I often lingered long enough that Julie Wallach, in her chef whites, would emerge from the tiny kitchen to say hello.

"I've been missing Little Giant lately as if it were a person," I wrote to Julie. "Thank you for creating such a warm and special place, and for hosting me and cooking beautiful and thoughtful food. The Little Giant menu has informed my cooking—I am always trying to recreate some of that magic. Jake and I will never forget when you sent a biscuit shaped like a VI for our sixth anniversary. We talk about it every year. Thank you. We miss Little Giant and YOU."

Julie responded with this email: "I don't think I've ever received such a touching letter before. Out of the blue and incredibly thoughtful. And so needed at a time when I'm struggling professionally. Your letter was a fabulous reminder that looking back is a good motivator for moving forward." Shortly thereafter, she announced that she was closing the Manhattan restaurant she'd owned and operated for the past decade, Tipsy Parson.

"I was super happy when we had Little Giant," she told me over the phone. "Everyone was coming together in a way that no one seems to do anymore. No one had their cell phones on the table. Tipsy Parson wasn't the same: I wanted to re-create the spirit we had at Little Giant, but the whole industry has changed.

"I opened your note at a restaurant near our house upstate. It was my husband's birthday, so we went out to lunch. I'd thrown a stack of mail in my bag, and I went through it while my husband was in the bathroom. I was in the midst of trying to sell Tipsy Parson. I'd moved upstate, but I didn't feel like I belonged there, because the restaurant trapped me in the city. I was sick with Lyme disease. I was miserable. When I opened your card, I remembered how happy I had been running Little Giant. I used to wake up and go to the greenmarket. And then I would send out food and see people's reactions from the open kitchen. I missed that connectivity. You get into the hospitality business to be hospitable.

"Getting your card, it made me look back and think, *I have contributed in some way to people's lives.* Because I wasn't feeling that way about myself at the time. It also made me a little melancholy: It made me think about all the people I have in my life that I care about. I loved running Little Giant, but all I did was work at that point. You and I, we could have been the best of friends. As you get older, you realize that time is the one thing you can't get back. And you start to feel rueful about how you spent it. I spent so much of my youth working in a basement. Hopefully I can make up for it now, in Julie 4.0."

Any Squirminess You Might Feel Is Unfounded

Julie's was one of many responses throughout the year that said something like, "I'm going through a tough time right now, and this helped." I was surprised to learn that a lot of people are going through something a lot of the time. I believe Julie felt comfortable opening up in such an intimate way because that's how I approached her.

It wasn't *cool*, what I was doing. I was putting myself out there, essentially saying, "Hi! It's been years, but remember me? Not only do I remember you—I think of you *constantly*." Someone who learned of the project said the thought made her feel "squirmy." "Isn't it awkward, reaching out to say thank you for something that happened years ago?"

Well, yes! Almost every note had involved bravery in varying degrees—a small bit with local shopkeepers; a bourbon shot's worth with friends who'd become estranged. Each of those notes felt like a small, achievable dare. It took guts to wave first.

It did get easier. The feedback I started getting—that I'd made someone's day, or made them smile—served as incentive. And anyway, I figured that the notes, no matter how random-seeming, no matter whether I felt awkward delivering them, would be well received. What I *hadn't* anticipated was that by making myself vulnerable, I was inviting others to do the same.

People overestimate the awkwardness of a heartfelt thank you, and they underestimate its impact. That's the upshot of findings by Amit Kumar, a social scientist studying gratitude at the University of Texas. Kumar asked four hundred participants to write a letter of gratitude to someone who had affected them and then studied the reactions of the recipients—something that was rarely done in the gratitude field. Most studies were solely about the benefits to the person who was feeling or expressing gratitude. Kumar focused on the impact.

"Your squirmy friend highlights a part of this that I think is super interesting—the fears of awkwardness that act as a barrier to expressing gratitude," Kumar told me. "Our findings suggest that people are inordinately concerned about what they're going to say, how articulate their appreciation will be, whether they'll get the words *just right*. These worries, we find, are overblown. Saying something, irrespective of precisely what words you happen to choose, can be meaningful."

This claim, Kumar added, "isn't opinion; it is a scientific fact: Sending gratitude letters will be far less awkward and more impactful than people think. Perhaps knowing that will be enough to help them overcome their squirminess."

I told Kumar about Julie's response and posited that if you time a thank you note just right, when the recipient happens to be going through a rough patch, it will mean even more to that person.

"I suspect that part of what you say is true, and part of it isn't," Kumar replied. "I am a scientist, remember, so I think about these things in the aggregate. I'm looking at hundreds of detailed responses, and there's very little variability. Virtually everyone says that receiving a gratitude letter makes them feel really, *really* great. Julie's reaction is typical, not atypical. The atypical part is that she gave you an accurate representation of how she felt."

Kumar pointed out that I wasn't following up with the recipients of thank you letters and making them fill out a questionnaire, as he did in his study. He insisted that if I did, I would learn that the notes meant more to people than I realize.

And that was why I kept it up, despite those hesitant thoughts that bubbled up: *How will this be received? Will Ruth Reichl think I'm lame?*

Honestly, who cared? It didn't matter what Ruth Reichl thought of me—it mattered what Julie Wallach did.

Expressing gratitude in this vulnerable, openhearted way is *not* cool. It's warm—disarmingly so. And that's what makes it powerful.

As I was mailing out my last food-month notes—a fan letter to Nigella Lawson, a note to my friend Teri about her pizza dough recipe—I thought about the question I posed at the outset of the month. Did thanking the people responsible for my favorite food memories reconnect me to my former food-loving self?

Maybe I wasn't the same foodie, but these notes reminded me that change is to be expected in the world of food. *Gourmet* is no more, and *Food & Wine* laid off just about everyone and moved to Birmingham, Alabama. All four of my favorite New York restaurants have now closed—Battersby and Prime Meats in the months since I sent those notes. Since cutting out gluten and dairy, I haven't been cooking much from Jenny Rosenstrach's cookbook; I haven't baked Diane's perfect hot cross buns from her handwritten recipe. As she wrote to me, neither has she. Magazines and restaurants are as ephemeral as food itself. But the taste memories remain, as do the people. They enhanced my life, and they are a part of me.

When I was starting to eliminate the foods I loved, friends kept offering their sympathy, wondering how I would manage without my beloved pasta, bread, cheese, and ice cream. I was surprised at how easily I adjusted, and in looking back, I give credit to my Thank You Year. I felt grateful for the health benefits I was experiencing. I felt grateful for the foods I could still eat (tortilla chips and Jake's smoky guacamole, French fries with mayo). I felt grateful for every bowl of spaghetti carbonara I ever ate. Every strand. Why do we feel entitled to every edible morsel on this planet, anyway, regardless of consequences to our body or the environment?

All of these food-related thank you notes inspired me to throw a last-minute dinner party, inviting people from disparate parts of my life and cooking them roast chicken with charred eggplant and green beans. I used tahini and anchovies that I purchased on my latest trip to Kalustyan's, the global grocery on Lexington Avenue, where I also bought preserved lemons and hot sauce made from Peruvian aji peppers. So maybe I'm still a foodie after all.

HOW TO IDENTIFY LIFE ENHANCERS

Maybe food isn't the thing that gives you daily pleasure. Try to find yours.

1. *Think about how you spend extra money or time.* If you found $10 on the street and had to spend it on something nonessential, what would you buy? You have one extra hour and can't spend it doing something productive. What do you choose to do?

2. *Ask yourself if there is something you never tire of talking about.* Perhaps it's comedy, or fashion, or weight lifting, or wine?

3. *Identify the potential note recipients.* Maybe you're involved in a community of people who like doing the same thing? How do you learn more or express your passion? Who have been your teachers? What did they say or do that you've never forgotten?

CHAPTER EIGHT

AUGUST: TRAVEL

How Writing Notes to World Expanders Can Lend New Perspective

SURPRISE: Travel creates lifelong friendships.

BENEFIT: Expressing gratitude extends a trip's afterglow.

LESSON: Travel changes you. No, really.

B ack when I was part of a skeleton staff launching Rachael Ray's magazine, my boss, Silvana, asked me what I'd want to focus on once we staffed up: Food news? Entertaining features? My answer came quickly: If the magazine had a travel section, that was what I wanted to run.

A few years earlier, when I was twenty-three and working as an editorial assistant at *O, The Oprah Magazine*, I took a magazine and newspaper writing class at the New School; the guest speaker one night was Salma Abdelnour, then the travel editor of *Food & Wine*. As Salma detailed the exciting food news coming out of southern Spain, a thought materialized, clear as if it were written in ink: I want her job. Like, *bad*. It was a clarification of my initial goal—to follow in Ruth Reichl's footsteps and write about food. I now wanted to follow in Salma's footsteps, writing about food trends around the world, getting paid to scout out the most exciting spots.

Editing the travel section of Rachael Ray's new food magazine was a step toward that dream, the start of a glorious ten-year stretch as a travel editor and world traveler. Working there, I wrote about celebrated American food destinations (Austin, New Orleans) and underrated ones (Walla Walla, Washington). I contacted some of my favorite writers and sent them around the country to sample the country's best barbecue and hot dogs.

After seven years, I stepped into Salma's former post at *Food & Wine*—I could hardly believe it!—and the destinations got farther afield and ritzier: New Zealand, Marrakesh.

It was difficult to square the person I was now—washing out sippy cups, cranking out SEO-primed content ("Does Pumpkin Pie Need to Be Refrigerated?")—with the globetrotter who attended conferences in London and Berlin and introduced celebrity chefs at food festivals in Mexico and Aspen. I was excited at the prospect of traveling back in time (so to speak) and reliving those fancy expense-account trips.

I know that my former existence is pretty unrelatable, and I'm not asking anyone to feel sorry for me because it's over. I didn't feel too sorry for myself: Even as it was happening, I knew those days were numbered.

Whenever Jake and I were enjoying some sort of outrageous job-related perk, one of us would quote Gael Greene quoting Julia Child. In a scene in Greene's memoir, the women were enjoying a lavish dinner at which the restaurant owners kept sending out one exquisite dish after another. When Greene expressed guilt, Child cried out, "I think we should just enjoy it! Who knows how long it will last."

While it lasted, though, it was a terrific privilege to get paid to travel—and not just travel, but experience different foods and cultures. Over the course of writing thirty-one notes, I realized that the lasting privilege wasn't so much the luxe hotels or frequent-flyer miles, now long expired. Writing these thank you notes helped me see that the years I spent as a travel editor taught me a people-first approach to travel that anyone can adopt. I practiced talking to strangers on trips, and that trained me to be comfortable doing so in my everyday life and especially throughout this gratitude journey.

Travel Creates Lifelong Friendships

I expected to spend this month recalling the sizzle reel of my past life, vacillating between savoring details of the lakeside lodge in New Zealand and erupting in fits of jealousy directed at my younger self.

I opened up a decades-old Word doc titled "Places I've Visited" and started annotating it with the people who made each trip great. Looking over the list of friends, tour guides, and PR people, I remembered a piece of travel advice that I often share: When researching recommendations before a trip, don't just ask, *Where should I go?* Ask, *Who should I meet?* Because a generous local is worth more than all the world's guidebooks and travel blogs and double-decker tours.

When I went to New Orleans to write a story for *Rachael Ray Every Day*, two PR agents named Kristian and Simone showed me around. I approach any PR person's tips with skepticism, knowing they have something to sell me. But Kristian and Simone were New Orleans locals, which meant that they were gracious hosts first and foremost. Kristian, who ran the tourism board, invited me to his house for a crawfish party. Restaurant publicist Simone let me tag along with her and her best childhood friend on their regular Friday lunch at Galatoire's (which was not a restaurant she represented). I fell hard for the city's Sazerac cocktails, and grilled gulf oysters drenched in hot sauce, and joyous second line parades. More than anything, I fell for the people.

"Dear Emery & Kristian," I wrote—including his wife. "I was just thinking about my trip to NOLA years back, and how you wonderfully warm & generous people welcomed me into your fold—from crawfish boil at your home to Jazz Fest insider's tour." And to Simone, I wrote: "I was just thinking about my trip to NOLA, years ago—and how generous you were to show me your insider's view of that wonderful city. Seeing Dr. John at Galatoire's was 100% priceless."

When I went to a travel conference in Berlin, I brought my sister, Brigitte, and we met up with Gisela Williams, a frequent *Food & Wine* contributor. After sitting by the fireplace in an impossibly cozy restaurant in her non-touristy neighborhood, Gisela introduced us to her friends Sharmaine and Alonso. They later walked us past a snaking line and into the opening party of a labyrinthian club vibrating with techno. The next night we drank wine together until 4:00 a.m.

"Dear Gisela," I wrote. "You were so generous with your time & introductions (to Alonso, Sharmaine). You made the city come alive as only a local can, and made me fall in love with it." To Alonso, I wrote: "You took my sister & me under your wing—got us into the coolest club, introduced us to Sharmaine, stayed up all night drinking & talking & eating." And to Sharmaine: "I was just thinking of you and our brief yet memorable times together in Berlin, London & NYC. I'm so grateful for our friendship—and looking forward to the next time we get to sit & talk & laugh."

I didn't line up a local guide before traveling to Austin to write a feature story for *Rachael Ray Every Day*, but I found one. One night, I was tempted to stay in my chilled-out hotel, the San José, and borrow *The Last Picture Show* from the hotel's DVD collection. Instead, I shoved my feet into just-bought Lucchese cowboy boots and headed out to South Congress Avenue. While I was eating a bowl of queso at

Güero's Taco Bar, a gentle-looking man named Russ sidled up and started chatting, and before long he invited me to see Austin legend Dan Dyer play at a nearby venue.

It's a paradox: Traveling by yourself opens you up to other people—not only meeting them and exchanging pleasantries but also befriending them. In the fifteen years since Russ and I tapped our boots along to Dan Dyer's music, we've seen each other a half dozen times, in Texas and New York and Massachusetts—he traveled there for my wedding.

"I was just thinking of the first time we met," I wrote to Russ. "How lovely of you to spot a girl out of her element and befriend her. You are such a special person—warm, open, generous. Thank you for showing me your Austin all those years ago—and thank you for all of your warmth & love & friendship since!"

These trips were short. I spent mere hours with Emery, Kristian, Gisela, Alonso, Sharmaine, and Russ in their hometowns. Yet a decade or more later, we're still friends. While reflecting on that, I was reminded of my conversation with Gillian Sandstrom, the author of the weak-ties study from my neighbors month. Sandstrom mentioned that she had pivoted from her weak-ties research and was now studying the fears around talking to strangers. "I've been trying to understand: What exactly are people worried about?" she said. "People really don't want to talk to strangers, for the most part. So why? What do they think is going to happen?"

I told her I was reminded of that squirmy feeling that people get when thinking about sending a random thank you note, the reluctance to wave first. "I think it's the same thing when talking to strangers," she said. "Almost all people feel that fear. But if they do talk to someone, they report back that actually everything went just fine."

Never more so than when you're traveling. Why does travel breed friendship? Maybe because it sets you off-kilter. You're out of your element, removed from your routine, which tends to pique your curiosity about your new surroundings. You engage more intentionally and intensely with the world around you. Maybe you listen better. Maybe you're quicker to skip past the surface and get to the more interesting parts of yourself.

While bonding with a stranger on a trip feels natural, keeping up those long-distance relationships takes effort. I invited Russ to Jake's and my wedding, for one thing. When I traveled to London for a long weekend, I skipped a half day of sightseeing to meet Sharmaine for oysters. And this month, I wrote them both notes.

I didn't end up spending much time yearning for the outrageous resorts I was lucky enough to visit. The work trips that made the biggest impact weren't the most luxurious ones—although sipping Champagne in a horse-drawn carriage at Ballyfin manor house in Ireland was pretty damn great. The most memorable trips were those on which I managed to make a true connection with a local. And that's something anyone can do at any time, in any town.

Expressing Gratitude Extends a Trip's Afterglow

Making a lasting friendship might be the best way to extend the life of a vacation. Are there other ways to stretch out travel's benefits (stress relief and creativity boosts among them)?

Studies have shown that the simple act of anticipating a vacation can lift your mood more than being on the trip itself. A University of Surrey study found that people are at their happiest when they have a vacation planned. They also feel more positive about their health and quality of life. Moreover, Amit Kumar, the gratitude researcher, co-authored a study that showed that we get more happiness from anticipating a travel experience than anticipating a new possession.

So you feel good when you're planning a trip—which ideally includes reaching out to acquaintances who'd be willing to meet up. But what about the aftermath?

In her book *The Myths of Happiness*, the well-known psychology professor Sonja Lyubomirsky wrote: "As we reminisce, a photo might remind us of a pleasant or funny detail we had forgotten, like the cute waiter who flirted with us or the rainstorm that drenched us. By paying concentrated attention to our momentary pleasure—say, as we reminisce about a long-ago vacation . . . we heighten our pleasure even more. . . . Mentally revisiting and relishing memorable experiences . . . can continue to generate happiness boosts for us even today."

If reminiscing about good times helps us revisit them, then writing travel-related cards could give new meaning to the idea of a mental health vacation—extending the pleasure boost to the card recipients as well. I met one of my closest friends, Grace, while we were both studying in Florence, but in different schools. I approached her at a nightclub, recognizing her from pictures that hung in my room the previous semester: Grace had gone to high school with my college roommate Alison. If I'd been afraid to talk to strangers, I would have never met my beloved Grace. To her, I wrote: "In a nostalgic mood & thinking back to our amazing travels when we were SO YOUNG & dancing on bars etc. Thank you for . . .

- ♥ Inviting me to the unforgettably lavish Ca'Vendri in Verona
- ♥ Navigating every trip in pre-smartphone days
- ♥ Escorting me to the Pisa airport to pick up my future husband
- ♥ Being the best travel buddy & friend imaginable. I LOVE YOU."

When Grace received this note, she was in the midst of breast cancer treatment (she is now in remission) and dealing with her mom's worsening health—all while mothering three young children and two dogs. She told me that she kept the note on her kitchen counter for a couple of weeks, and every time she spotted it, she felt a surge of happiness, remembering our weekend in Verona and our late nights in Florence. Then she put the card away in a memory box, she said, where it sits waiting to give her pleasure at some point in the future.

This month taught me that writing a note is the simplest, surest way to extend a trip's joy—something that I confirmed on a shave-ice-fueled family trip to Maui (the result of a barter with a hotel client on the island). Once home, I sent out six thank you notes. To Jen Murphy, my predecessor at *Food & Wine*, who sent along a long list of perfect Maui recommendations: "I was constantly toggling between your articles and cheat sheet."

To Jen's friend Amanda, who lives in Maui's Upcountry and who texted me recommendations in real time: "It was thanks to you that we went to the Mill House (twice!) and Ululani's. YUM!" To my childhood friend Garrett, who's now living the dream as a fisherman on the island, I wrote: "MAHALO for taking the time to meet me and my family, and for making us the best poke we had all week!" It was snowing in Brooklyn, but I could almost feel the Maui sun as I wrote.

On that vacation, I had no article to write, no panel to moderate, no advertiser to glad-hand. It would have been easy to kick back at the Grand Wailea, riding the waterslides at the resort and rarely venturing beyond its gates. But I still travel like an editor, which means I want to see a place through the eyes of the people who know it best, and I want to meet those people.

The thank you notes have solved a problem for me. Formerly, I would thank my travel helpers, but casually, either via email or text. I always had a nagging feeling that my quick text wasn't quite sufficient, and I'm sure along the way I forgot to thank someone who sent a list of recommendations or hooked up a reservation. Writing notes that detail specific ways that a person improved my trip feels like a proper acknowledgment of their time—with the added bonus of stretching out those good vacation vibes.

Travel Changes You. No, Really.

"Travel changes you," said the late, unbearably great Anthony Bourdain. "As you move through this life and this world you change things slightly, you leave marks behind, however small. And in return, life—and travel—leaves marks on you."

I held the assumption that my travels had influenced the person I'd become. I wondered if this month would illuminate how, exactly.

I thought back to the memorable trips of my youth and thanked my dad and my childhood best friend's dad for their two very different travel styles.

"Dear Dad," I wrote. "I was just thinking of all the little trips we took when we were kids—when we would jump in the car without much of a plan or reservations of any kind . . . and find ourselves in San Diego or Reno or wherever you thought of. Thank you for teaching us to love travel & to have adventures & to value beautiful views & starry nights. . . . Thinking, of course, about when you got us out of bed to look at the incredible stars on a clear night in . . . where, Yosemite?"

To my best friend's dad, I wrote: "Dear Mr. Goddard (I'm nearly 40 yet you'll always be Mr. Goddard!): I was just thinking about the wonderful Goddard family trips to Lake Tahoe. Thank you for always making me feel so comfortable & a part of your family—in your house and on the road. I remember you putting on Bob Dylan & John Denver & we'd all sing along."

My dad's last-minute trips had instilled an appreciation for adventure—and an anxiety about showing up without reservations. In stark contrast were the vacations I took with the Goddards, who rented out a cabin months in advance, scheduled outdoor activities each day, and played charades every night. I saw there was comfort in a structured itinerary. From the back seat, I took in these two travel styles, my dad's and Mr. Goddard's, and when I grew up and moved into the driver's seat, I melded the two.

One trip springs to mind. A writer acquaintance, Veronica Chambers, offered Jake and me her Paris rental for the week. I planned out our itinerary to the minute, but we ended up abandoning most of those plans—including a side trip to a castle in the Loire Valley—because we were so content hanging around Veronica's neighborhood, the Marais. While in Paris, Jake proposed the ultimate adventure. "Dear Veronica," I wrote. "We are coming up on 12 years since our incredible week in Paris, when we got engaged. How generous of you to lend me your charming apartment, having barely met me once or twice. It was the ideal place for such a key moment in our lives. That trip remains our favorite-ever vacation. It was magical & so memorable start to finish—and you had a lot to do with that."

I later assigned Veronica an essay about the time she surprised her husband with a birthday trip to Tokyo; they stayed at the Park Hyatt, the hotel from *Lost in Translation*. Veronica's article made the city sound at once stimulating and peaceful, and while editing the piece I told Jake that we weren't going to have kids until I visited Japan.

Two kids later, I was offered a spot on a small press trip to the iconic Park Hyatt Tokyo. I had never taken a press junket, though I'd been invited to plenty. I preferred to travel on assignment, not owing anyone any favors or coverage. But. This was my chance! Not only to finally visit Japan but to temporarily reclaim the globetrotter identity I'd lost after leaving *Food & Wine*. Jake agreed to take over all kid responsibilities while I was away. I practically skipped aboard the Japan Air plane.

I raced through Tokyo—I recommend spending more than three days—and now, the memory that's the clearest is the afternoon I spent with Yukari Sakamoto, *Food & Wine*'s Japan stringer and the author of *Food Sake Tokyo*. "I was just thinking of our afternoon," I wrote to her, "and how generous you were to 1) send me all of your best Tokyo tips, 2) give me a tour of the depachika, 3) eat noodles with me." In the "depachika," the food-filled floor of Takashimaya department store, Yukari pointed out miniature cherry cakes and other hyper-seasonal treats. Hydrangea was in bloom, and the blowsy blossoms covered nearly every box of chewy mochi or elaborate pastries. In the coming weeks, Yukari told me, all of the hydrangea packaging would be gone, replaced to reflect the season. It was the kind of detail I'd never have known if I'd walked the floor by myself. I bought delicately crisp, soy-glazed rice crackers in a purple hatbox covered in the exact kind of pink hydrangea I had seen for the first time in a botanical garden earlier that day. How lucky Japan was to have this uniquely beautiful flower, I thought.

Two days later, when I wheeled my luggage down our Brooklyn walkway, I couldn't believe it—there they were, that exact type of hydrangea, also pink. It was our first summer in our new home, so each month brought new blossoms that we hadn't seen before. They were glimpses into the future, when we might snip a peony for Henry's tenth birthday party, or collect spray roses for a summer dinner party.

The metaphor was obvious. At this exact stage in my life, I didn't

need to board a transatlantic flight to find beauty and adventure. There it is, in the everyday details, if I look. Travel changes your perspective, just not always in the way you expect.

Looking over all the notes I wrote that month, I felt overcome with gratitude for the parts of the world I'd been lucky enough to see, and for the people who'd helped me unlock their treasures, and for the friends I'd made. I would take incredible trips again, and meet more fascinating people who change my perspective, even if I wasn't doing so right now.

I also felt grateful for the small ways that travel had changed me. I often return from a trip pledging to make some tiny life alteration. Keep poetry books accessible on low shelves. Take a walk after dinner. Wander into an art gallery. All of these little declarations share the same basic purpose: Slow down. Look around. Take it in. Writing thank you notes has become my way of accomplishing those ends.

Later on in my Thank You Year, my mom unearthed an old journal that I kept on my semester abroad in Florence, when I was twenty. Here's an excerpt from the last entry.

> Jon and I walked home along the river, stopping at my favorite place to sit and watch the Ponte Vecchio. We talked so much about Florence—how we may be the most "ourselves" than ever before, maybe ever after, because we've had no real scholastic distractions, very few friend/family/boy problems to deal with, and really only this city and the others we've visited to think about.

We *are* the most ourselves when we travel. Maybe it's those run-ins with our truest selves, even more than the places we visit, that change us.

HOW TO WRITE POST-TRIP
THANK YOU NOTES

1. *Collect recommendations from people you trust.* In order to have people to thank after your trip, you're going to have to ask for a few favors. You can ask friends who have visited the destination recently, but a local is ideal. Social media is, of course, a great way to locate those people. It's good to be as specific as possible about what you're looking for: a reasonably priced hotel in a central location, a solid restaurant in the theater district.

2. *Plan to meet up with a local.* This could be someone you grew up with or a friend of a friend. You might feel uncomfortable asking someone you don't know well to meet up. But imagine the possibilities! You could uncover the city's greatest steak or make a friend for life. And people love showing off their town.

3. *Chat up everyone*—the cabbie, the waiter, the people standing behind you in line. Ask them specific questions: Where would you go for lunch in this area? Do you have a favorite pizzeria? What museum shouldn't we miss?

4. *Exchange email addresses.* If you make a real connection with someone, jot down their information.

5. *Write thank you notes once you return home.* It doesn't have to be right away—your note will be appreciated even if it arrives years later. Share detailed memories of the time you spent together and what it meant to you.

CHAPTER NINE

SEPTEMBER: CAREER

How Writing Letters to Mentors Can Boost Confidence

BENEFIT: Expressing gratitude is the most authentic way to network.

LESSON: There is no statute of limitations on a thank you note.

SURPRISE: Reconnecting with mentors can lead to unexpected career twists.

For fifteen years, I climbed the glossy ladder of my magazine career. Sure, the perks were great—the travel opportunities, the restaurant opening parties, the beauty closet sales where Chanel makeup went for $1. But what I loved best was collaborating with uncommonly talented writers, art directors, publishers, and fellow editors on a product we all cared deeply about.

That collaboration was what I missed the most since leaving my job at *Food & Wine*. After surviving two rounds of layoffs, I was felled by a third. As I walked out the revolving door into the bright sunlight on Sixth Avenue, awkwardly clutching a serving platter that was too delicate to messenger to my house, I recalled sauntering into the building through those doors on my first day, feeling giddy that I had finally landed my dream job. And I wondered, what was my new dream?

I was still trying to answer that question three years later. Working for myself—I'd learned that the term sounds less frivolous than "freelancing"—had its your-time-is-yours advantages, but there were plenty of disadvantages, too, the primary one being that *there was no ladder*. It was just me, floundering, trying to find purchase in a world that no longer paid writers a premium for reporting or editing articles. I'd enjoyed some wins—working with national brands like Boll & Branch, publishing a stylish cookbook about nachos—and some major losses, like pulling in a third of my magazine editor salary the previous year.

As I prepared for my next month of thank yous, I wrote "Career Mentors" at the top of a blank page, then bristled at the word "career." Did I even have one anymore?

Expressing Gratitude Is the Most Authentic Way to Network

I figured I'd have to get creative to come up with a month's worth of mentors. While some of my magazine friends had jumped from masthead to masthead every year or two, reporting to a myriad of bosses along the way, I had worked at only three in fifteen years, five if you count internships. And now I was my own boss.

I went through my résumé, starting at the bottom with the internships, and thought back to each office, identifying people who taught me something. I couldn't believe how fast the piece of paper filled up. That was the first surprise of the month—how many people had helped lift me to where I was, ambivalent as I felt about that place.

One of my first and best mentors has been Frank Lalli, the former editor of *George*, who pulled me in to help launch Rachael Ray's magazine, and who had been a sounding board and confidant ever since. I looked at a blank card and starting thinking about all the ways he'd been generous with his time and advice over the years. There were so many, though, that I once again broke my no-outlining rule, grabbing a Post-it and jotting down a brief timeline of every instance he'd helped me.

I saw that this month's approach would have to be different. When writing to a neighbor or a doctor, two or three detailed and heartfelt sentences felt just right. With mentors, though, I wanted to share more—why I was writing now (often a decade or more after we shared office space), what I remembered from our time together, how they had influenced me. These would be more like letters, and some would need to be outlined beforehand. And they would take longer to compose than four or five minutes each. But, as I soon came to learn, that time and effort paid back tenfold.

I started my note to Frank, the platonic ideal of a mentor, then used it as a template for most of the others: "I've been looking back on my magazine career . . ." And then I got specific. "You hired me at *George*, giving me my first NYC internship. You gave me so much of your time that summer—encouraging me to pursue a story lead and contribute ideas. It was my first exposure to the glittering (at the time!) magazine world." A number of densely written paragraphs later, on the back of the card, I signed off with, "I can't overstate how grateful I am for your years of mentoring. You're the best of the best."

I soon received a reply in the mailbox. "You're too generous," Frank wrote. "From where I was sitting, I saw an extremely intelligent young talent with ideas, principles and drive. So I hired you as many times as I could. Editors do that. We're talent scouts of the young and proud mentors of the adults our best hires become. I couldn't be prouder of you."

It was the first of many mentor responses that gave me a much-needed boost of confidence and the feeling that, while I may spend my days sitting by myself at my computer, I am not alone.

I wrote to my very first magazine boss, Lia Haberman, who hired me as an intern at a long-defunct teen magazine in Southern California called *MXG*: "I'm so grateful that you gave me a chance to write; that you took the time to explain how a magazine is made; that you made NYC sound cool. Thank you for being so nice to that 20-year-old beach kid." She DMed me: "It meant so much more than you know and came at a time when I really needed some positive feedback." I remembered the lesson I learned during my food month, that a lot of people are going through something a lot of the time. A codicil: Magazine people have an increased chance of being in a downswing.

Speaking of which. I glanced at the top of my résumé, to *Food & Wine*, and I thought of my mentors there. The obvious choice was Dana Cowin, the former editor in chief who hired me. But she also laid me off, and I couldn't bring myself to thank her for it. It still felt too raw. I thanked two former *Food & Wine* coworkers as well as Salma, who inspired me to be a travel editor, and quickly moved on down my résumé.

I thanked five coworkers from *Rachael Ray Every Day*, and in doing so I remembered specific traits that I'd admired and still emulate. To Rachael Ray herself I wrote, "Everyone who knows you describes you as smart & hard-working, and it was incredible seeing for myself how right they were." To Bonnie Kintzer, then a vice president who owned every room she walked into, and now a CEO, I wrote: "I remember overhearing a tough phone call with [redacted] where you gave it to her straight and thinking—Bonnie is a total badass. I will always try to emulate you when I need to come across as confident, fearless, capable, smart." To Courtenay Smith, the executive editor who exhibited calm under pressure, I wrote: "You were always so unflappable—you mentioned your meditation practice, and that made sense to me. It was a strange time at the magazine—high stress, high stakes—but you were a force of sanity and calm." To Theresa O'Rourke, Courtenay's hilarious and sharp predecessor, I wrote: "You gave me confidence in my own voice and skills. And you made coming to the office so much fun." And to the talented and hardworking Maile Carpenter, the magazine's founding executive editor, I wrote: "I admired your decisiveness and saw how important that quality is in a boss. You taught me so much about food writing, and about finding the most fun way to tell a story."

I took all those lessons with me, and though I am not the big boss at a magazine, as I once hoped, I still use the skills these women modeled.

Maile, now the editor in chief of *Food Network Magazine*, replied with this email: "I just got your note and it made my day/week/year. Truly. What an amazing letter to find in the mail, and the feeling is mutual. Those really were the good old days!" We caught up the following week at the classic Pearl Oyster Bar, and she later wrote about our meal as part of her *New York* magazine Grub Street Diet, a column where notable people journal their food for a week. "We grabbed a tiny table by the window," she wrote, "ate bowls of New England clam chowder and shared a lobster roll and a pile of shoestring fries while we talked about the good old days in publishing. On nights like this, I feel like I've lived in New York forever, and I never want to leave."

When I turned to *O, The Oprah Magazine*, my first full-time job, I was surprised at how many mentors I listed: eight—more than at any other publication. It was so long ago—before kids, before marriage, before smartphones—and I wasn't even an editor yet, but a lowly assistant. As I wrote those letters, I realized that my years at *O* were truly formative. I started to see a direct line between that job and this project.

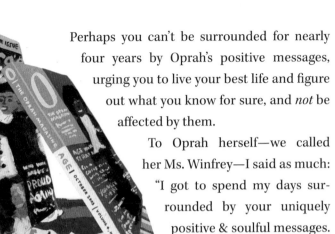

Perhaps you can't be surrounded for nearly four years by Oprah's positive messages, urging you to live your best life and figure out what you know for sure, and *not* be affected by them.

To Oprah herself—we called her Ms. Winfrey—I said as much: "I got to spend my days surrounded by your uniquely positive & soulful messages. I remember at an all-day convention you urged us to 'listen to the whispers,' and I've tried to do just that ever since. Thank you for treating me to dinner at the Four Seasons, and for flying me to Chicago for your birthday. Seriously, how spoiled was I?" To her best friend, the talented journalist Gayle King, I wrote: "I admired how you treated each person at the office the same. You always had time to say hello and smile—even years after I left the magazine, when I ran into you at the cafeteria."

My first two immediate bosses were opposites in almost every way. To the warm, funny, easy-to-please Lisa Kogan, I wrote: "How lucky was I, a 21-year-old newbie to the city, to be gifted you for a boss? (Very!) I loved that you offered recommendations for restaurants and hairdressers as well as the recipe for your dishwasher salmon. You brought so much fun & life & kvetching to the office."

Lisa gave me lessons in kvetching. One Monday morning she asked how my weekend was. "Great!" I chirped. "Well, I got food poisoning Saturday night. Aside from that, it was great." She stared at me over her cluttered desk. "Stop," she said. "Start over. Repeat after me: *I had a terrible weekend. I got food poisoning.*"

And to my other boss, the stricter, more easily exasperated Mary, whom I lived in fear of but eventually won over (I think?), I wrote: "I know when I arrived as a 21-year-old newbie, I was entirely green and clueless. I am grateful you didn't fire me! I saw in you a role model for hard work and accountability, and I tried to step up to that example."

To Catherine Kelley, the former executive editor, I recounted: "I will never forget standing in my new, empty Herald Square apartment (ha) when my Nokia phone rang. You sounded thrilled to offer me my first full-time job. I think I screamed?" And to the then editor in chief, Amy Gross, I wrote, "Thank you for reading & liking & publishing my essay about being 24. It was a career highlight."

I clearly remembered details about the process of writing that piece: reading the soon-to-be-published essays from writers of varying ages for the upcoming age-themed issue; interviewing those authors for the contributors' biography page (including the incredible Anne Lamott); holing myself up in my studio apartment all weekend to write the twenty-something perspective that I felt was missing; dropping that unsolicited draft in Amy's inbox early Monday morning. I didn't remember much about the essay itself, as it had been published more than a dozen years ago. I dug the magazine out of my closet and reread it. Funny enough, thank you notes played a role.

Now, two years past graduation, it seems the SATs begat college exams, which in turn begat the real test. Here's what I've gathered: Success will not come because I'm ambitious and desire it, but only after much, much, and more hard work. Mistakes I make have weight, and my fallback phrases of "I forgot," et al., don't count as sound reasoning. (No excuses.) Being kind far outweighs being interesting. A strong woman can—and should—be tactfully honest rather than brutally blunt. (Watch your mouth.) It's imperative to recognize people's needs, return calls, be trustworthy, and show appreciation for the regular outpouring of love I'm shown. (Send a thank you card.)

What would that twenty-four-year-old make of my life now? I wondered. She'd be relieved to hear that her home life was happy, that she'd married the college sweetheart who made her laugh, that they had two little boys. As for my career . . . She'd first need to be caught up on the state of magazines—that interns were no longer feted with lavish goodbye parties at sushi restaurants, as she had been in 2000; that not every editor had a dedicated assistant, in fact most magazines had only one; that many of her favorite magazines had folded; that writers were paid less than the $2-per-word fees she helped shepherd through at *O, The Oprah Magazine* in 2003. After learning all of that, I think she'd understand my exit. She'd be disappointed that I never published the novel she was bragging about writing in her bio note. I don't think she'd like some of the assignments I'd been saying yes to—the SEO articles about whether you should refrigerate pumpkin pie. I think that wide-eyed optimist would encourage me to keep trying to write something bigger, something deeper, something better.

Writing letters to mentors had clear, immediate benefits—more, perhaps, than any other month so far. It had led to conversations, not only with my twenty-four-year-old self but also with former bosses and colleagues. I'd stumbled upon the most authentic, generous method of networking. Why aren't more of us doing this?

Is it because of—and I'm sensing a pattern here—the perceived awkwardness?

There Is No Statute of Limitations on a Thank You Note

During my food month, I contended with the squirmy feeling you have to overcome when sending a card to someone you haven't seen in years. That feeling was ever present as I was writing to incredibly busy, successful people—CEOs, television stars. Would they find it weird that I was referring to things that happened so long ago?

Thank you note etiquette rule number one almost always involves timing—that notes should be sent out within a week or two, and always within a month. And for a standard thank-you-for-the-gift note, or a more formal thanks-for-the-interview note, a quick turnaround makes sense. But a full nine months in, I understood that what worked for those transactional notes didn't apply to more enduring expressions of gratitude. For those thank yous, a delayed letter *means more.*

"That's what made the note stand out, how out of the blue it was," said Chandra Turner, a career coach and the founder of media networking site Ed2010, to whom I'd written: "You've spent so much of your time trying to connect and help people in our industry—while it was thriving and once it was tanking."

Because Chandra helps so many people land jobs, she has "a giant basket of thank you notes," she told me, but, "no one writes to you years later to give an update."

That's a missed opportunity, according to the organizational psychologist and bestselling author Adam Grant. "The impact of mentorship is hard to see in the moment," Grant has said. "It only unfolds over time." In a tweet from 2018, his advice is explicit: "When you receive great advice from a mentor, don't just send a thank you note the next day. Send another the following month or the following year. The passage of time shows deeper gratitude and more lasting impact."

More than just four-by-six proof that your mom taught you manners, a delayed acknowledgment shows that this person's words and deeds not only resonated in the moment but also continued to influence your life. The delay turns the card into a surprise, a little gift unto itself.

Reconnecting with Mentors Can Lead to Unexpected Career Twists

Once I'd written to all the mentors from my magazine years, I turned to these past three years of self-employment. I was my own boss, yes, but were there people who'd offered guidance?

Yes, there were. I wrote to Nick Fauchald, whom I'd met in the early days of launching Rachael Ray's magazine and who'd become a dear friend: "The conversation we had when I was laid off from *F&W* was the first time I felt like, OK, I can do this. Then, you convinced me to write the cookbook that made my parents and everyone in my hometown proud."

I'd told my friend Cara that I was interested in content marketing, and she promptly introduced me to her friend Rod Kurtz, who showed me the ropes. "I was so entrenched in the warm bath that was my magazine career, and so intimidated by what I felt certain should be my next step," I wrote to Rod. "But what was content marketing, exactly? And what was a KPI? Why is everyone saying ROI? You were so kind to explain it all to me."

And I thought back to my dad, who had built a successful small business. "You are my most important mentor," I wrote. "Growing up, your dedication to growing your business made a big impression—how you were always on the lookout for leads wherever we went. Jotting down phone numbers as trucks went by. And you always emphasized the importance of being your own boss and making your own schedule. I've so often thought of your advice that 'sales is just a numbers game.' Thank you for laying the groundwork and always supporting me and believing in me."

While writing these final notes of the month, I was getting more responses from my magazine mentors, learning how they were dealing with the industry carnage. Lisa, my first boss, was still working at *O, The Oprah Magazine* three days a week, and she'd also started ghostwriting books and speeches for celebrities. She went on to say, "But enough about me . . . okay, one more thing about me: every time I see your name in my inbox, I feel like I've won some sort of a prize. And your card was really about the nicest thing I've received all year. Gina, you always had my back and I can't tell you how much it means to know that despite all the years apart—you're still there."

Catherine, who'd called to offer me my first job, had been a fan of my Thank You Year since I told her about it in July, when I emailed to ask for contact info for her friend, the cookbook author Jenny Rosenstrach. Catherine was now a VP at Yaddo, an artist residency program. She invited me to lunch, and as we sat eating sushi, she wondered if my Thank You Year could turn into a book. The thought had occurred to me, but it felt vague and pie-in-the-sky. Hearing Catherine suggest it made the possibility seem real.

Catherine also asked me about my content marketing clients. As I answered, casually dropping terms like "biz dev" and "ROI," I felt that it was time for me to take my content marketing business seriously. I needed to get comfortable defining the term "content marketing" without cracking a joke that the job sounded fake. So what if it did! This was now my career, and it was time I treated it as such. My company had a name—Penknife Media—but not a website. Later that day, I reached out to the graphic designer whose contact info I'd had on a Post-it for months. I commissioned her to design my company a logo, and then a website.

Around this time, I got an email from Jenny Rosenstrach. She thanked me for my note and asked for details about the gratitude project, which Catherine had told her about. Jenny wondered if she could perhaps write about it for the blog she contributed to, Cup of

Jo. Jenny interviewed me and wrote a post titled "A Year of Magical Thanking." Before it went live, I started an Instagram account dedicated to the project—ironic, considering I began my Thank You Year as a way to step away from Instagram—and posted pictures of each batch of notes so far.

Both the article and the Instagram account elicited enthusiastic responses from readers, and I started interacting with those people, experiencing social media's best and most powerful purpose: finding a like-minded community.

It made me think: Could this hobby evolve into a new stage of my career? On January 31, when I had counted up my thirty-one City Harvest cards and hatched the idea for this undertaking, was that one of Oprah's whispers? Would it possibly lead to something beyond 365 cards? Spoiler: It led to this book.

A year and a half after my month of thanking mentors ended, I ran into Dana Cowin (my former boss at *Food & Wine*) and decided to write her a thank you note after all. "I loved seeing you a couple of weeks ago. Thank you for being so enthusiastic about this gratitude project and book. This thank you note is belated by a year or two: I thought about writing to you during my Thank You Year, but I guess I wasn't quite past your laying me off, despite the years that had passed, and despite the tumultuous fall of magazines in general. (AKA I'm in good company.) But seeing you reminded me of all the ways you've been supportive of me over the years. I want to thank you for hiring me—that was my #1 dream job since meeting Salma in my early twenties. Though it only lasted three years, I remain humbled & grateful for that opportunity. My world opened up when I got that job. I worked with such crazy talented people, in the office and around the globe. Your high expectations made me a better reporter, editor and writer. Thank you for helping me grow. Thank you for giving me a shout-out on the editor's page—what a thrill. Thank you for assigning me feature stories once I left the fold. Thank you for continuing to be a cheerleader. You were a mentor then, and you remain one now, and I'm grateful for it all."

Her response: "I am so grateful for the note you sent me a bit ago . . . The honesty of sharing that you weren't quite over the hurt and the magnanimity of putting it aside many years later moved me to tears. I've carried the note on planes/trains/autos, waiting to get a sec to write back on paper. I kinda gave up on that. So here I am. Thank you. Really. Thank you. You were super talented back in the *F&W* days and I hated to lose you from our team. You had a unique and valuable perspective. Those staff cuts were the beginning of the end for us. I've watched with joy as you've thrived . . . built a business . . . been an inspiring leader/mom/human."

As wildly uncomfortable as it makes me to relay her compliments, I do it to show that expressing appreciation can heal wounded relationships, and egos as well. When in doubt, err on the side of gratitude.

HOW TO WRITE GRATITUDE
LETTERS TO MENTORS

It's the most generous and authentic way to network.
What are you waiting for?

1. *Think before you write.* While I generally advise a loose
   approach to thank you notes, letters to mentors (who might
   have helped you in many ways, at different times of your
   life) often call for a little more planning. In the words of
   one of my mentors, the editor Susan Chumsky, "The most
   important part of writing is thinking."

2. *Explain why you're writing.* A good way to start is to
   explain in brief why you're reaching out now, perhaps years
   later. Here are some of the ways I started my letters: "Maybe
   it's because I'm approaching 40, or because I've transitioned
   out of magazines—in any case I've been looking back to the
   earlier part of my career and thinking about you," "I've hit a
   little milestone—four years since I left my last desk job—and
   I've been looking back and thinking about the people who've
   helped along the way."

3. *Recall how the person helped you.* This could be advice
   they gave, introductions they made, or the example they
   modeled. As always, the more specific the better.

4. *Mention their long-term impact.* Perhaps they changed
   the course of your career or said something that you think
   about nearly every day. Bring their long-ago mentoring into
   the present.

CHAPTER TEN

OCTOBER: BOOKS

How Writing Fan Mail Can Reconnect You to Yourself

BENEFIT: Writing to your idols reminds you who you are.

SURPRISE: Sometimes they write back!

LESSON: Librarians and teachers are the real heroes.

They say you should never meet your heroes. You can, however, write them a letter.

My books month would be made up entirely of fan mail to authors. For a New Yorker, trained to look *away* from celebrities on the street, to give them their space and avoid fawning at all costs, it was uncomfortable to imagine. But I'd already sent my first-ever pieces of fan mail in July, and writing to my favorite cookbook authors and food memoirists hadn't felt as cringey as I'd feared. I wasn't bothering someone at the airport to ask for an autograph. I was simply offering talented people my admiration, sharing my experience with their work, and thanking them for it.

But I worried that dedicating a whole month to writing to strangers would feel cold and detached and, frankly, boring in comparison with the deeply personal interactions of past months, which had forged new ties and repaired old ones.

Writing to Your Idols Reminds You Who You Are

In October I took myself out to lunch, sat by the window, and turned to the task of listing my favorite authors. I unfolded a brown paper napkin, and my pen hovered. So many names flew into my head. Jane Austen. Roberto Bolaño. Toni Morrison, Willa Cather, Edith Wharton, Gabriel García Márquez, Wallace Stevens, Mary Oliver. The first, most obvious challenge was that dead writers can't receive mail. Another issue materialized: It was intimidating to settle on a list of all-time-favorite authors. I knew I would obsess over it, revising and overthinking, which would prevent me from writing the actual notes.

I overcame this obstacle by rethinking the list: Instead of "Favorite Authors," I titled it "Books I Loved." Identifying thirty-one of those, and thanking their (still breathing) authors, seemed manageable. I wrote fast, thinking of books that I'd read in the past few months (*The Bone Clocks*, *The Guernsey Literary and Potato Peel Pie Society*, *Homegoing*, *Educated*, *A Little Life*, *Between the World and Me*), series that I adored (Harry Potter, His Dark Materials), and childhood loves (The Baby-Sitters Club). I jumped from genre to genre, from mystery (anything by Tana French) to memoir (Patti Smith's *Just Kids*) to manual (I was an early Marie Kondo adopter).

By the end of lunch, I had a first draft—which I did revise, but not obsessively. I crossed off Elena Ferrante's Neapolitan quartet and Donna Tartt's *The Goldfinch*, as the former writer's true identity has never been revealed, and the latter novelist is famously reclusive.

That night, after the kids were in bed, I wrote my first letter to David Mitchell, about his novel *The Bone Clocks*. I tried to describe why I loved it. "The quick plot, rich characters, imaginative premise. I hate sounding like a generic book review—but please know that reading this book was pure pleasure."

Well, that could have gone better.

I tried again, turning to the book I'd read just prior: *The Guernsey Literary and Potato Peel Pie Society*, by Mary Ann Shaffer. I held the novel in my hands, paging through it, thinking about why I'd enjoyed it. I reread the afterword, which explained that the author had died before finishing the book, and so her niece, the writer Annie Barrows, had completed it.

"Dear Ms. Barrows," I wrote. "I'm writing to tell you how much I adored *The Guernsey Literary & Potato Peel Pie Society*. It was a pure delight to read. It had been years since I felt this type of lighthearted joy while reading. I loved reading your afterword almost as much. Thank you for bringing your aunt to life in such a crystal-clear way. I loved hearing about her 'willingness to be delighted by people.' I'd like to think I have that quality, and I believe that it's the best part of me."

When I wrote that line, I felt that tingly sensation that comes when writing is *working*, and realized what would become this month's North Star: Fan mail should be *personal*. Not necessarily for the recipient's sake, but for mine. I knew that some of these letters would get stuck at agents' offices or in a slush pile, even if their authors weren't recluses. Would J. K. Rowling read my note? Was Polyjuice Potion brewing in my bathroom? No! So what was the purpose of writing to her?

"Harry Potter has given me so much over the years," I wrote. "Here's a little timeline." I went on to mark the year I started reading her books (2001) and the year I stayed up all night racing through *Order of the Phoenix* instead of unpacking boxes in my brand-new studio apartment (2003). In 2008, "my sister and I threw the first of two 'Harry Potlucks,' in which we screened all the movies (that were out at the time) from 7AM–midnight. People came through all day long, bringing pumpkin pasties or 'Cornelius Fudge.'" I marked the years when the audiobooks eased an onerous commute, and when the Broadway show anchored the perfect New York City day with my sister and best friends—and signed off with, "Thank you for sharing your beautiful imagination and talents with the world. It has brought me endless joy." I almost added one last bullet point, a hopeful note for the time when I'd read the books to my sons. But I didn't want to jinx that decades-long dream.

I mailed the letter to the address listed on Scholastic's website, understanding that it would never reach J. K. Rowling. The letter had already served its primary purpose: It had allowed me to revisit my relationship with her work, and to honor it.

With this in mind, I went book by book, rereading passages, thinking about why I loved the stories in the first place and how they had affected me over time. And when I wrote the letters, I kept this directive in mind: *Make it personal.*

To Patti Smith, whose very name made me smile with affection, I wrote: "*Just Kids* is a treasure of mine. I keep my copy at my in-laws' house in the Berkshires, and I pick it up when I have a quiet moment. I love getting a glimpse of my city before it was mine. I love how you spend the book honoring people—Robert Mapplethorpe, of course, and also your parents and yourself. Thank you for working so diligently to honor your art and creativity. P.S. I missed your reading at St. Ann's because my four-year-old was wailing for me not to leave. (He was still getting used to life as a big brother, and was extra needy.) I hope to hear you read in the future."

I picked up another beloved nonfiction book, *Between the World and Me.* To Ta-Nehisi Coates I wrote: "I know nothing about what it feels to be you, the man, or you, the father. I live with so many fears about my kids—thank you for illuminating me to yours. I will read your book to my boys when they're older. Thank you for sharing your perspective. Thank you for your gorgeous writing."

I stacked up the manuals that have informed the way I parent, eat, drink, and organize. To Pamela Druckerman, an American expat and mom in Paris, I wrote: "*Bringing Up Bébé* was such a breath of fresh air amid the stale, boring baby books I subjected myself to in my oldest's first year. I think about so much of the advice so often. I think about how you should give your kids multiple opportunities to like a new taste. My husband proposed in Paris, so it felt joyful incorporating these aspects into my parenting."

All the way back in 2006, before "free-range" or "grass-fed" had entered the public lexicon, Jane Goodall, yes, *that* Jane Goodall, wrote *Harvest for Hope*, a prescient mindful-eating call to action. To her I wrote: "It's crazy to think that just a decade ago, I hadn't spent much time thinking about the provenance of my food. And I worked at a food magazine! Reading your book changed my shopping and eating habits for life. I still visit my farmer's market every week, and plan my family's meals around the produce I pick up. Thank you for being so far ahead of the curve, and for sharing your point of view."

I wrote a similar note to Barbara Kingsolver about her local-food memoir, *Animal, Vegetable, Miracle*, telling her that I read it "in my since-disbanded food book club. I don't know if all book clubs end, but mine certainly have!"

I confessed to Bianca Bosker, the author of *Cork Dork*, about my many failed attempts to become proficient in wine. "I've wanted to learn about wine over the years—I took classes while studying abroad, and in my early 20s. But so little stuck. And then I started working at *Food & Wine*, and I felt so out of league with the wine pros. Reading your book taught me so much about wine, and it was such fun to read. It's clear how much work went into it—thank you!"

Writing to Marie Kondo was oddly emotional. I pretended we were sitting down to tea, a translator between us, and told her about my Thank You Year. "I'm wondering if the whole project started with reading your book," I wrote. "I Kondo-ed my stuff when my son was one and a half, and I was recently laid off from my job. I was transitioning from that first year of parenthood into my new normal life as a mom, while pivoting my career. Your process was cathartic, and I loved what I was left with—items I truly treasured. Now that I'm nearing the end of my thank you note project, I'm realizing that I've organized my memories in a similar way to how you helped me organize my stuff. I'm cutting through the noise and junk to honor the most precious people and memories—and in doing so I'm honoring my own life."

I spent some time retrieving memories from the beginning of my journey as a reader. In the second grade, I read my longest book to date: *Heidi*, a hardbound covered in a tactile navy fabric. I finished it while lying on my Laura Ashley pink tulip bedspread. *I* wanted to one day write a book, I thought, holding *Heidi* in my hands reverently, but I couldn't imagine typing out all the words on all those pages. I started small, writing little stories in cursive in tiny pink notebooks.

Then I devoured book after book: *Little Women, Island of the Blue Dolphins, Matilda, The Secret Garden.* In the fourth grade I discovered the Baby-Sitters Club series, which I couldn't get enough of. Like so many kids across the country in the late eighties, I tried to start my own babysitter's club, along with my friend Katy.

To Ann M. Martin, I wrote: "Okay. The Baby-Sitters Club was EVERYTHING to me when I was 9–10 years old. I'm nearly 40 now, and I can still remember how excited I was when a new book arrived (via mail, because I ordered from those forms at the end of the book!). These books were such a comfort to me. I loved reading about the solid friendship these girls had. I loved how smart they were, and industrious. I related to Mary Anne's shyness, Claudia's artsiness, and Stacey's family situation (her parents were divorced, I think?). I always liked reading, but this series clinched it for me. Thank you for inventing this world and for writing these books."

It was actually Dawn with the divorced parents. If some details were hazy, what remained clear were the feelings that the series evoked in me.

I wanted to foster that same love of reading in my kids. I wanted them to find the books that they'd stay up late reading, books they'd hold close. For that reason—and because I was always on the lookout for ways to teach Henry gratitude—I pulled him into this process. The fact that dictating eleven thank you notes to his favorite authors took as much time as writing one of mine—that was just a bonus.

Some Heroes Write Back!

Henry was game for the challenge. I asked him to pull his most cherished books off the shelves, and he got to work on building his stack. I gave him only a little guidance—nixing the Golden Book version of *The Lion King*, proffering (but not pushing) a few of my favorites.

We sat at the kitchen table, and one by one, he dictated his messages of thanks to the authors (first and last names, he insisted). He added his shaky signature, next to which I jotted down his age—5.5 years.

"Dear Kadir Nelson," he said. "I love you because I love *Baby Bear* because it's really beautiful. I love the way you painted the moon."

"Dear Dev Petty, I love you. And I love *I Don't Want to Be a Frog* because I love the pig and everything else. It's funny for me. It makes me think about frogs. The wolf is a little nice to frogs because they're too slimy."

"Dear Joshua David Stein, I love *Can I Eat That?* because it's really funny. I know all of the words. I love the sea urchin part—and then I went and ate some. So that makes me really happy. I liked eating sea urchin. I have a question for you—Do you like to eat doughnuts?"

We ended with the book that we reference nearly every day, which Henry explained: "Dear Audrey Penn, I love *The Kissing Hand* book because it always makes me happy. When I'm sad it makes me feel better. At school I give my little brother, my mommy and my daddy a kissing hand. And they give me a kissing hand so I can feel happy at school."

Without my explicit direction, Henry understood what I'd learned about writing good fan mail: It should be personal. And perhaps the intimate nature of the notes, short as they were, moved some of the writers to respond.

Dev Petty sent a package with a frog sticker that she signed with a heart; five bookmarks emblazoned with a frog saying, "What am I doing in this book?"; and this handwritten letter: "Dear Henry, Thank you so much for getting in touch! I'm so happy you enjoyed Frog. He's a fun guy to write because he's silly but asks a lot of big questions. . . . Sort of like me! I also like PIG, he makes me smile. Happy Reading! Your pal, Dev."

family favorites

Thank You

fan mail

author responses

The Kissing Hand's Audrey Penn wrote back with a typed letter explaining the origin of her raccoon mother-and-child story:

My son was just a little younger than you are now when we spent the day at our favorite park. The first thing we did was buy tickets to ride the red choo choo train that travels throughout the forest. Our ride was almost finished when the train stopped because an animal was resting on the railroad tracks. I thought it was a deer and when the conductor left us to get a park ranger, I tiptoed to the front of the train to take a peek. I was quite surprised to learn it was a huge mother raccoon that was holding us up, not a deer at all. I tiptoed backward in order not to scare the raccoon that was actually scaring me. My eyes were cast downward and that's when I saw the baby cub. Later I learned that the baby was one month old. I watched the mother raccoon take her baby's hand and open it wide. She bent down and kissed the cub's palm, leaving her scent on his hand. The cub then put his hand on his cheek. A moment later, the tiny raccoon reached over and gave his mother a Kissing Hand of her own. It was a truly magical moment. I hope you and your family have a wonderful holiday season and continue giving each other kissing hands. Thank you again Henry, for your very thoughtful note.

Lots of hugs,

Audrey Penn

Enclosed is a copy of *Chester Raccoon and the Almost Perfect Sleepover* and a book about having a younger brother called *A Pocket Full of Kisses*.

Henry was, naturally, thrilled to receive presents in the mail. When I read him Audrey Penn's letter, he listened in rapt silence, for once not fidgeting with his cuticles or sleeves. When I was done, he kissed me in the center of my palm—that was a kissing hand. I asked him how the letter made him feel. "It makes me feel like doing kissing hands more," he said. "And it makes me really happy that we are kind of in touch with some book people."

Receiving the packages underscored that there are people responsible for the things we love. Giacomo Bono, the co-author of *Making Grateful Kids*, had told me that making that connection was key.

As for my authors, very few responded, as I'd predicted. Bianca Bosker emailed me a lovely reply: "I just wanted to send you a very (*very*) belated thank you for your kind note, which meant so much to me to receive. Thank you for reading *Cork Dork*! I'm honored to hear that it helped shape your wine journey, and appreciate you taking the time to write to me." And I received polite and appreciated form responses from Jane Goodall and Barbara Kingsolver.

The responses were nice, but the true benefit of writing fan mail was realized in the writing of it. Communing with beloved books reconnected me to perhaps my truest self, the reader that was born on that tulip-printed bedspread.

When we're kids, we fall in love with our favorite books, songs, movies—wearing out the tape, writing down the lyrics, waiting in line the day it debuts. Those pieces of art imprint themselves upon us and help us define who we are. The passion might dilute with age, but the impressions remain—if we take the time to look. Writing to authors reminded me that I am still capable of loving books in the same tender, earnest way I had as a child.

Librarians and Teachers Are the Real Heroes

While social media is a slippery-slope addiction, occasionally it can be a beautiful connector of people. Two weeks after I started my Thank You Year Instagram feed, I received this DM: "Thank you for the inspiration. I'm a high school librarian & today was our first Thankful Thursday. Students could come to the library during their lunch & write a thank you note. All supplies were provided & library staff are delivering notes for the students. It was an awesome 1st day!!"

Immediately I wrote back, elated and requesting more details. Thus, I began my correspondence with the librarian Beth Mulch of T. C. Williams High School, a massive four-thousand-student high school in Alexandria, Virginia.

A few months later, Beth shared that teachers had started "inviting me into their classrooms to bring thank you card writing to their students." She sent me pictures of the high schoolers sitting around a table, hunched over their thank you notes, faces intent with concentration. Who were they writing to? I wondered. Did some students come back to Thankful Thursdays at the library week after week? Were they feeling the same benefits I was?

I asked Beth if I could come to the school to find out. After receiving permission from the principal, she invited me down for a visit, timed to the day when the criminal justice teacher was bringing in her students for a thank you note writing session.

I decided to take Henry along as a reward for all his help. We took a train to D.C. and a cab to the high school, where Beth met us at the front door with a huge smile. Outside the library was a sign reading "Thankful Thursdays."

Inside was a wooden table covered in cards and pens and a poster board asking, "Have you thanked someone lately?"

Beth introduced me to Kris Gulden, the teacher whose twelfth graders were just starting to file in and sit down on stools around small tables. "Hey, everyone, good morning," Ms. Gulden said. "Earbuds out, phones off, computers off."

Beth spoke to the students, explaining that the Thankful Thursday program started after she read the Cup of Jo blog post about my Thank You Year. Beth admitted that most students started out skeptical. Ms. Gulden had hosted a class here before, Beth recalled, and said, "I'm going to be honest: My feeling from the class initially was a lot of *Uh, really, are we doing this?* But by the end of it, most people wrote not just one card."

Beth explained that the library team would hand-deliver the thank you notes addressed to students and teachers. She uncapped a pen and asked the students to brainstorm people to thank. On a whiteboard, she jotted down the words they were shouting out: "friends, teachers, coaches, parents, sig. others, tutors, role models, siblings, coworkers, someone you haven't seen in a while, janitors, bus drivers, religious leaders, community leaders."

One girl suggested, "People who work in the cafeteria because, oh my gosh, the disrespect!"

Another said, "Are you throwing Ms. Gulden on there?"

"No!" Ms. Gulden said.

The students helped themselves to cards and pens and started writing.

I walked around the room, Henry trailing me *very* closely. I approached a confident-seeming student who had smiled at me encouragingly when I introduced myself to the class.

"Who are you going to write to?" I asked.

"All of my teachers," she replied. I asked how many, and she said eleven.

Impressed, I left her to it and walked to another table, where I spotted an envelope that read, "To My Homie."

"Who's your homie?" I asked.

"My friend since elementary school," a boy in a cap said. "He always pushed me through school when I didn't want to do it. In ninth grade I did not want to go to school at all. So, he would come to my house because we live one street apart. He made sure I got ready for school and made sure I actually went to school. I thanked him for keeping me in school and getting me through school."

"Have you thanked him before?" I asked.

"I have thanked him by just saying it, but I think with a card it means more. Because written things you can keep forever, I guess, and words you can easily forget. I feel like it would be more important."

A girl ran up to our table and presented a card to a boy who'd just written her one. "I'm going to write you a real one," he said. "The last one was a joke."

Another girl told me she was in Ms. Gulden's class for the Thankful Thursday session last year. "After that," she said, "I wrote some thank you notes to some of my church members. I thanked them for being there, for caring, and for praying for me."

I spotted a girl racking up a whole stack of cards. She pointed to a friend sitting next to her and said, "I wrote one to her. I wrote one to Ms. Gulden, and one to a friend who lives in North Carolina. I'm writing three more to some of my other friends. I'm kind of on a roll right now. I think when I started writing about my friends, I was like, I have a lot to be thankful for. A lot to thank them for. I might as well share my appreciation to as many of them as I can."

I asked the first girl how far she'd gotten in her goal to write to all eleven of her teachers. "I'm actually still on my first one," she said, "because I am writing a really long one for Ms. Gulden. Honestly, I'm just talking about how being in her class has changed my life. Because before I took this class, I had no idea what I wanted to do with my life. But now I know I'm going to study criminology, and go into the FBI, hopefully. I'm also talking about how she puts a lot of focus on making sure our mental health is in a good place. She's always there to talk to us if we need anything, and she teaches us important values and things that are going to help us throughout life, not just in high school. It's been a really beneficial overall class. I never had a teacher like her, and I probably won't again."

A lot of the students were thanking Ms. Gulden, I discovered. One girl confided what she was writing: "I feel like no one had faith in me that I could, like, *be* somebody, but she did, since last year." Then she said, "I hate this school."

"Why?" I asked.

"There are too many people; it's too crowded in the hallways; people stare. It's too much for me. I am a people person, but at school I am just quiet and to myself. But Ms. Gulden is someone I want to honor. If I come back, she's the first person I'll come back to because she's really had a big impact on how I view things. In the real world, it's going to be hard. And she didn't sugarcoat it. Her advising me on stuff, it really made me think. And now I'm not *ready*, but I'm ready, if that makes sense."

I wandered over to Ms. Gulden and asked why she'd brought her students here. "It's a nice diversion from the academics," she said. "Everyone needs a break. We spend so much time on testing, and I think some of the daily life skills and taking care of each other emotionally is overlooked or lost. We have a lot of kids who have home problems. Two kids recently dealt with deaths, and there are family issues and college applications. It's nice from time to time to be able to take a step back and say, let's do something else, something that makes us feel good."

Before the class was dismissed, Beth told everyone to write the recipients' names clearly—first and last names—and add them to the basket. The library staff would deliver the notes later that day.

"We put them in teachers' mailboxes, and there's no acknowledgment of where they are coming from, or why," Beth explained. "Someone last year found me and said, 'I had come to work one morning feeling not necessarily at my best and not wanting to be here. But I went to my mailbox, and here all of a sudden was this note out of nowhere.' It just changed the course of that person's day. How amazing is that, that a student sat here and wrote a note, and how that ended up inspiring someone. I love that. I love putting these notes in all the mailboxes, not knowing what's going to happen for the person that day."

A woman named Laurel, who was manning the front desk, added: "I think Beth created a culture where thank you notes are common. I have gotten more from other teachers, and I am more likely to write them. I just had a teacher leave a little gift on my desk. I was like, 'Why did you do that?' And she said, 'I just think you're nice!' So I stuck a note in *her* box. I think this program at the library has fostered that culture."

When the bell rang, a half-dozen students handed Ms. Gulden their notes on their way out. The one who hated high school said, "I'm going to fail twelfth grade so I don't have to leave you."

Ms. Gulden replied, "You've meant a lot to me, too."

As another set of students filed in with their lunches, and some sat around and started writing cards, I asked Beth if she'd noticed any other benefits throughout the course of the program.

"A student has said, 'I have never received a thank you card before.' And through this being a part of our school culture, they received a card. That moment was really impactful for them.

"And," she went on, "some students at first think they don't have anyone to thank, and then they realize that they do. I think that's beautiful. That's a life lesson: Step outside whatever you are in, and realize what you are appreciative for."

As Henry and I were getting ready to leave, Beth handed us a card that she had written surreptitiously while we were talking to the students, which thanked me for giving her this idea in the first place, and thanked Henry and me for traveling all this way.

That afternoon, Henry and I sat on the train bound for New York. I had planned to write a few thank you notes—a train is the ideal place, after all. Instead, we raised the partition between us, snuggled together, and spent the entire ride reading *Harry Potter and the Chamber of Secrets*.

"I think Voldemort is the one who opened the Chamber of Secrets fifty years ago," he whispered to me.

"You're right!" I told him, too impressed to play it cool.

"Really?" he said, his voice creaking with pride. "My teacher said good readers guess what's going to happen next."

"You're going to be a *great* reader, if you want to be," I said, silently thanking Henry's first-grade teacher, Ms. Bruno, for this moment.

HOW TO WRITE GOOD FAN MAIL

1. ***Identify the art you're passionate about.*** Maybe it's not books; maybe it's music or theater or movies.

2. ***Write a list—quickly.*** Instead of ranking your favorite albums or plays or shows, jot down what comes to mind first.

3. ***Revisit the material.*** Go back to the source and remember why you loved it.

4. ***Make it personal.*** Even though you're writing to a stranger, you can still speak from the heart, adding specific, personal stories and feelings.

5. ***Find an address.*** The person's website often lists an address—either for the author, or for their agent or editor. If there's only an email address, send a note asking for the best mailing address.

CHAPTER ELEVEN

NOVEMBER: FAMILY

How Expressing Gratitude to Family Members Can Improve Your Relationships

SURPRISE: Sending holiday postcards extends festive feelings.

LESSON: Expressing gratitude disarms and leads to change.

BENEFIT: Thank you notes can build trust.

With just two months left in my Thank You Year, I was feeling both excited and exhausted. My career and books notes had been more like letters, longer and more detailed than any other cards I'd written throughout the year, and I'd completed them all while taking on new clients and assignments.

With the holiday season approaching, I could feel anxiety creeping in like muscle memory. November would be filled with family events, which meant packing, preparing, party throwing. We would visit my dad for Veterans Day and then welcome my mom for Thanksgiving—a holiday whose history leaves me cold, but whose gratitude association I appreciate. For the past seventeen years, I've loved spending Thanksgiving at my in-laws' apartment, but this year it was being renovated, so we were hosting for the first time. I'd also invited my mom's side of the family over for a post-Thanksgiving Sunday brunch.

And when that two-party weekend was over, instead of recuperating, I would immediately prepare for Christmas and Hanukkah and New Year's. How would I write the rest of my thank you notes amid the craziness?

I spent the previous year's holiday season feeling overwhelmed, irritated by the trappings that had once delighted me. When I found myself sitting on a quiet train car to New Jersey in January, the silence and solitude felt like the biggest gift of all. That I was wasting it on my social feeds led to my launching this project.

This year, I hoped that the ten months I'd just spent immersed in gratitude would translate to a more positive, relaxed approach to the holidays. I wanted to enjoy the season and recapture some of the magic it held for me as a child.

As for my family-themed thank you notes, I had a plan to make them more manageable.

Sending Holiday Postcards Extends Festive Feelings

At this stage of my Thank You Year, I had become fairly adept at figuring out the best format for a batch of recipients. When envisioning how to thank family members, I knew it would be too intimidating to write thirty overarching gratitude letters. I imagined writing to my mom, selecting from countless moments, thanking her for making me milky tea, and for editing out the dirtiest parts of *Dirty Dancing* on VHS, and for, I don't know, giving me life? And for, like, everything else?

The prospect of such meandering letters reminded me of my friends month, when I had turned old pictures into "Remember When?" postcards. The picture inspired the content, as well as a dose of nostalgia, and the limited space made the task doable. I *couldn't* write an exhaustive account of our relationship even if I wanted to.

For the family batch, I could have looked through old pictures, but I had another idea. I would see so many family members this month—why not document our time together and turn *those* pictures into postcards? The instant memorabilia would double as holiday cards.

And, bonus: I wasn't able to write these cards until the very end of the month, after all the celebrations, which gave me a little breather.

The family month kicked off on Veterans Day, when Jake, Henry, Charlie, and I flew to Florida for a long weekend with my dad, his partner, my sister, and my brother, all of whom I was careful to snap pictures of.

When we returned home, I went into full holiday mode, prepping for my mom's arrival and the back-to-back Thursday and Sunday Thanksgiving and brunch parties, both of which were terrific, thanks in no small part to all the guests who pitched in.

I made sure to take plenty of group photos—something I never remember to do and always vaguely regret—as well as some more intimate shots, of Charlie kissing my uncle's bald head, of cousins lounging on the couch, barefoot and sated, with Henry sleeping between them.

Capturing these sweet moments with family members I see only once or twice every year or two gave me a new perspective on the holiday. Instead of running around, I was *looking* around. I was watching for special moments to capture, and therefore I saw them. Mentally, I was already writing these notes, spotting the people who were clearing plates, or playing with my kids. It was an entirely different approach to hosting, one that forced me to be rooted in the gathering instead of simply producing the party.

Writing out the thirty postcards at the end of the month didn't feel like a chore. Partly this was because it was less of an art project than my postcards to friends had been. I printed out the photos on heavy card stock (I used a company called Artifact Uprising), eliminating the need for mailing label reinforcement. All I had to do was draw that vertical line with a message on the left, the stamp and address on the right.

I started with the Veterans Day pictures. "Dear Brigi," I wrote to my sister, on the back of a shot of her with the kids and their pretend rocket ship. "Thank you for playing with my children in a cardboard box for hours. Your patience for them and deep, deep love for them is a gift, and really kinda knocks me out. Thank you for being such a great aunt." Jake had taken a picture of my dad teaching Henry to fish. "Thank you for keeping an eye on the boys," I wrote. "They adore you—I do too!"

Among my Thanksgiving batch were notes to my in-laws, thanking them for "essentially catering Thanksgiving," and one to Jake's cousin

Gary for the "delicious sweet potato pie! I ate some for breakfast the next morning." And I thanked members of my Italian family, including my aunt Mia for bringing her delicious meatballs and sausage to Sunday brunch, my cousin Jen for being so great with my kids, and my cousin Marie for bringing her "fun energy and dirty jokes."

I'd learned in my travel month that sending out thank you notes after a trip extends its glow. Similarly, sitting with pictures and basking in gratitude for these family members—for their helping out or for their showing up and being themselves—enhanced and prolonged the good feelings the holiday gave me.

That's right: My holiday season launched with a lot of good feelings and minimal anxiety. I felt markedly less overwhelmed and melancholy than the previous year. Whether the existential dread and panic stayed away through New Year's, that remained to be seen.

Expressing Gratitude Disarms and Leads to Change

I sent my mom not one but three postcards. In the first picture, she's sitting with my brother at our Thanksgiving table, which was set with the lace tablecloth her aunt made and lined with linen napkins and branches that my sister foraged in our front yard. I wrote: "Thank you for traveling to us for Thanksgiving—it was a wonderful visit. Look how cute you look here! :) Wishing I look half as cute at your age (48, 49?)." On the reverse side of an action shot where she's talking with big gestures, I wrote, "I appreciate how engaged you are with everyone." And on the back of a family group shot from our brunch, I wrote, "Thank you for being such a huge help all week—setting up for the party, cleaning up, etc."

In my friends month, I sent my best childhood friend, Katrina, three postcards from three stages of our friendship—at ages eleven,

sixteen, and twenty-two—because I couldn't pick just one. I sent my mom three postcards for a different reason, and not (only) because I started running out of family members. For her, the three cards—which I sent out three days in a row so she could have a little surprise in her mailbox for three straight afternoons—were a way for me to emphasize how much I appreciated the effort she put into this trip.

My mom had last visited in May, for Mother's Day, when I'd planned for the two of us to sneak away for a quiet breakfast at Cantine, the local café whose owner I'd written to in my neighbors month. I was excited to spend time alone with her, without children hanging on us, for the first time in I'm not sure how long. Instead of bonding, though,

I found myself shouting at her across steaming mugs of tea and plates of fluffy eggs, while she looked around the small room, embarrassed.

I'd rather not get into what she did to upset me. Imagine *your* mother. Imagine something she does that gets under your skin—not only gets under your skin but sort of festers and burns your insides. Now imagine she does that very thing—which by now, for God's sake, she should know drives you insane—during the tiny window of time you have alone together.

Like most people, my mom doesn't appreciate being yelled at in public, so our May visit never recovered from Brooklyn's worst Mother's Day breakfast. But unlike most people, my mom has an ability to not only forgive but also to reflect on her own shortcomings and make real change. Between her May and November trips, over a few phone calls, we dug into the crux of what had bothered me that morning, and she really listened.

Naturally, I was anxious about her November visit. Would we show each other our worst of selves once again?

Right away, she addressed the festering-under-the-skin issue and told me her plan for avoiding it. As her first day became her second and then her third, I felt my body relax. And then, holiday task by holiday task, greeting one person after another, I stopped thinking about it.

During Thanksgiving weekend, while I was documenting the parties and recognizing the best in each family member, I was also cataloging everything my mom was doing: coloring with the boys, washing every dish, folding every shirt, and even, hand over heart, making our beds. I wasn't only filing these acts away silently, waiting to write them down—I was voicing my appreciation.

Being mindful of and grateful for my mom's efforts, and everything that's charming and unique about her—how she notices someone's new haircut; how she can strike up a conversation with absolutely anyone; her affection, her warmth, her unending optimism—helped the friction fade and then disappear.

For my mom, receiving praise for what she's doing right allowed *her* to relax. We enjoyed each other's company in a way we hadn't in years. The visit went so well that I invited her to join our upcoming family vacation to Maui, the one I earned with my copywriting services.

It was not easy to switch my mind-set. What had the weak-ties scientist Gillian Sandstrom said? "We have strong ties, and they matter the most." She'd gone on to say: "They are the most important things for our happiness, our social relationships. But they are a lot of work." *This* was the work. But ten months of deep-gratitude immersion had been my training. Gratitude helped me arrive at a place where I focused not on what my mom wasn't but on what she was.

It was more than forgiveness that I was experiencing. That Thanksgiving week I realized something that I've been trying to hold on to ever since: that my parents gave me everything they could, everything of themselves, and that it is my job to fully accept them, and love them as they are.

The debt I owe my parents is so immense, so all-encompassing, that it is hard to acknowledge. It's like being grateful for air. Every morning on her birthday, Patti Smith says a prayer to her parents, thanking them for her life—something it hadn't occurred to me to do until then.

When I was a kid, if my parents agreed to buy me something frivolous, I would hide behind a rack of magazines or clothing as they paid for it. I was hiding from the thank you I owed them. I felt embarrassed. It's so much easier to take things and people for granted—

especially your family members. Moms in particular get the best and the worst from their kids. I see it with Henry and Charlie. They save their sweetest and most terrible behavior for me, taking my love for granted because they know it will always be there (even when they're asleep).

When Henry was a baby, an app called Wonder Weeks would inform me about each emotional milestone. One week, it buzzed to notify me that Henry was just then realizing that I was a separate person from him. There was a time when my children saw me as an extension of themselves, instead of another human being. My actual humanity was taken for granted, and sometimes still is. And maybe I'm guilty of the same.

An hour or so after my mom had arrived for Thanksgiving, she pulled out of her luggage a palm-size shiny leather notebook embossed with "Firenze" in gold letters. Only as I paged through it did I remember: I had written her a letter every night of my semester in Florence as a thank you. She had paid my tuition and boarding at a time when she really couldn't afford it. The journal was essentially one long thank you note—a precursor to this year—that doubled as a twenty-year-old time capsule.

Reading through, I was struck by the tenderness of those letters. It was a strange feeling, like I was peeping on something intimate that wasn't meant for me. I didn't talk to my mom the same way anymore. Could we recover any of that intimacy?

My mom had bookmarked a page with a picture of me at four years old, wearing a pink sweater and holding my Raggedy Ann doll. She read the passage aloud, her voice creaking in parts: "I wish I had a closer relationship with Nonni and Grandpa, speaking of regrets. It's hard, though, being so far away. I suppose that was really tough for you, twenty-five years ago, making that decision. I hope I never have to make it. Let's make a pact: Always in California. Or you move to live near me (*vicino a me sempre, certo?*). I want my kids to know you well."

My mom is currently hatching a plan to move to New York.

So, thank you, Mom, for giving me life, first and foremost. And then, for making sweet, milky tea for us to drink while we watched that VHS tape of *Dirty Dancing* where you edited out all the R-rated parts. And let's not forget when the airline wasn't picking up the phone, so you drove to the airport to stand in line and rebook my flight. Thank you for anticipating everyone's needs by keeping not only tissues and Band-Aids in your purse but also, inexplicably, nude fishnet stockings. And for, like, everything else.

Thank You Notes Can Build Trust

One of the most life-altering benefits of my Thank You Year has been improving relationships with my closest family members, who received multiple cards. My sister and brother showed me kindnesses throughout the year, and each received a handful. My father-in-law, Andy, and brother-in-law, Teddy, were also frequent recipients. My dad fit into almost every month's topic. He was a parenting helper, travel inspiration, career mentor, and provider of food (he sends regular shipments of the Meyer lemons and avocados that grow in his yard). I thanked him for contributing to my City Harvest fundraiser in January and, during my health month, for surviving a heart episode.

And then there was my mother-in-law, Lu. Ever since February— when I wrote her a note the same day I thanked the cashier from Trader Joe's—I'd regularly slipped cards into her red tote bag on the Mondays that she and Andy watched the boys. I wrote Lu a total of eight notes. Some were off-topic, acknowledging all that she had

Things I Thanked My Mother-in-Law for This Year

helped us with—buying Henry a winter jacket and knock-knock joke book and magnetic tiles; sewing the odd button; quilting us a table-cloth; dropping off Tupperware containers of salmon patties and chicken paprikash; baking Jake's favorite (labor-intensive) rainbow cookies—and some were on topic, like the time I thanked her for an impromptu therapy session in my health month. Lu is a gifted ther-apist and, therefore, an excellent listener. I always feel better after unloading my thoughts and worries onto her.

I already knew that Lu was a particularly helpful mother-in-law and grandmother—none of my friends' in-laws double as nannies once a week. But cataloging *everything* that she does for us was powerful, because, as I wrote in one note, it made me feel "so taken care of."

But I wondered if Lu saw things the same way. She agreed to sit down for an interview on a Monday morning before picking up Char-lie at school. A few days before we were set to meet, she left me a long voicemail. When I spotted it, I worried that she was nervous about the interview and was calling to bow out. I pressed play.

"I've been struggling with wanting to tell you this, and I guess I want to tell you it before I see you on Monday," she said, "because I don't want this to distort all the positive impact of all your thank you notes, of which there have been many. And maybe I got spoiled by getting them. But I felt badly that I didn't get a card from you for my birthday. I know this weekend was important in so many ways, but I guess I sort of imagined on the airplane or something, there would have been time to write me one of your notes. So I wanted to tell you that. I know you didn't do it to hurt me or anything like that. But it just . . . it did hurt me. And I guess I felt a little neglected in that way."

Ugh. Lu's birthday had been the previous week, and the boys cel-ebrated with her while my siblings and I were visiting my dad for the weekend. She was right: I meant to bring a card with me on the plane and forgot, and then the birthday came and went and I let it slip by, with only a perky text message to mark the occasion. I called her right back and left her a message, apologizing that I hadn't prioritized her birthday as she had always prioritized mine.

Lu arrived early for our interview, and thanked me for my voice-mail apology. We hugged and sat down at the dining room table, mugs of ginger tea in hand. I asked for her perspective on all the thank you notes, and she said, "I felt like you were remembering all these things that I felt like I had long forgotten. *Oh yeah, I did all that!* I would think. I was amazed at how much you observed and remembered, and it was clear you didn't feel intruded upon in your life, and *that* felt good."

"You had that worry?" I asked, surprised. "Like, maybe Gina doesn't want this, or this is too much, or something?"

"Yes," she said. "My mother-in-law, Andy's mom, would call up and say, 'I made a brisket, could you come over?' It was using food in that kind of way. I think I lumped the whole thing together, feeling controlled and intruded upon by her.

"In meeting you years ago and seeing that your relationship with Jake was going to be a permanent one, I was mindful of not wanting to repeat those mistakes, and always feeling a little cautious. I wanted to have a relationship with you, which I never really felt I had with Andy's mom, even though I felt she approved of me. What we're really talking about here is transference."

"Can you define 'transference' for me?" I asked. (Here was where Lu's profession came in handy.)

"Transference is when early-life relationships, usually with one's mother or father or siblings, get transferred. You put your experience with those people onto somebody else. You make an assumption. It's very often unconscious," she clarified. "People are reacting to a person as though they were their mother or their father, and they are so *sure* they are going to act in a certain way. It's hard work to become conscious about that assumption, to think, *Who was like that in my past?* I try to get patients to start thinking like that, and it's difficult.

"Like, after you and I had that argument years ago," she said—I knew the one she meant—"I assumed that you were going to bear a grudge because that's what I experienced from my mother. You're seeing somebody through a veil of what was in the past, and you're not seeing them for who they really are. So you transfer onto them unhappy experiences that really don't belong with that person."

I asked Lu how receiving these cards helped her let go of any transference she had with me.

"I always felt thanked and appreciated by you, first of all, even before the cards started," she said. "But the written word is a fixative. Words, when they are spoken, can sort of float away. But the written word is clear. There's no ambiguity. The sentence is the sentence. And so, reading those words becomes reparative."

Lu tried to remember an example, and I showed her photographs of a few of the notes I'd written to her. She put on her glasses and read one aloud: "'And just for constantly thinking of our needs.' It's the words, Gina. It's so helpful."

I asked Lu if she still has that apprehension around me, like maybe I still find her gifts of food or clothes intrusive.

"I don't think I have it anymore," she said. "It's not even I *think*, I *know*. And I can't tell you exactly at what point it changed. But it took time to really believe that you were who you were, and believe what you said, and to develop that trust. The notes were very reassuring to me, that I wasn't too much."

I told Lu that since writing the notes, I felt more emboldened to initiate difficult conversations with her and Andy, because if anything little came up, I'd think, *I just thanked them for a dozen things, so I can address this little issue.* "I knew you wouldn't take it as if I was complaining about lots of things," I said.

"You were really brave to bring things up," Lu said, "especially as the person who is not blood-related in this situation. I think it was so important. Getting things out in the open has been so helpful. I do think that the cards helped. After a conversation, if there was anything left over, the cards were reparative."

I told her that I felt our relationship had never been stronger.

"It probably has been that airing of the conflicts," she said, "plus the cards that have been forming a more solid foundation of trust. Clearly, I knew and trusted that I could share my feelings about my birthday card. To me, that was a sign that so much transference had gone away and that I really trusted you. I think the cards played a part in that. You responded to my message right away, and I couldn't have asked for more."

We hugged, and, as I was gathering my things to leave, Lu started folding our laundry, as she does every Monday.

HOW TO SEND POST-HOLIDAY POSTCARDS

1. *Take lots of pictures.* Capture the candid moments, and gather everyone up for a group shot.

2. *Make note of everyone's contributions.* Who is washing dishes without being asked? Who is playing hide-and-seek with the kids? Who brought a nice bottle of wine?

3. *Print pictures onto thick card stock.* I used Artifact Uprising.

4. *Turn pictures into postcards.* All it takes is one vertical line and a postcard stamp.

5. *Write short, specific messages* thanking people for their particular contributions to your holiday—their gifts, their jokes, their time.

CHAPTER TWELVE

DECEMBER: LOVE

How Writing Real-Life Love Letters  Can Bring You Closer Together

BENEFIT: Expressing gratitude can strengthen your bond.

LESSON: Gratitude is contagious.

SURPRISE: Giving up your power can be the ultimate power move.

'd written Jake five thank you cards so far this year—for taking the kids to his parents' one weekend so I could work; for organizing my lovely birthday picnic. This month, I would write Jake a thank you card every day.

The idea seemed to strike a chord with people, and not necessarily in a good way. At karaoke with Jake's work friends, I heard a few variations of "Why doesn't my partner do that for me?" My dad said, "Wow, Jake is one lucky guy!" The subtext was, I wish *I* was as thoroughly appreciated. Everyone used a joking tone, but behind it lay an unmistakable truth. This grand gesture, thirty-one thank you notes from one spouse to another, made people uncomfortable and put them on the defensive. *Should I be doing something like that for* my *partner?* I imagined them thinking. And then, *Wait, why is thanking them* my *job?*

Why isn't it theirs? That line of thinking is one I was familiar with and something this process helped me to overcome.

Expressing Gratitude Can Strengthen Your Bond

Somehow I managed to keep this month's theme a surprise from Jake. Getting into bed on December 1, he spotted a note on his pillow and, smiling, ripped it open. "Thank you for picking up the Christmas tree and setting it up today," I wrote. "December is . . . too busy. Thank you also for talking me through my anxiety when my to-do list is too long—which it definitely is all through the holidays. I love you."

Jake gave me a kiss. The next night, he didn't seem all that surprised to find another card on his pillow, thanking him for "telling me to stay out with Laura and the gals, despite your being covered in Charlie's vomit. I definitely would not have been so generous." I think he imagined that by then I was growing tired of finding gratitude recipients outside our home. Also, he had just dealt with our kid's vomit—dude deserves a thank you.

It was on the third night of December, when Jake spotted a card in that same spot, that he knitted his brows together, looking at me curiously.

"You're my December theme," I said.

And so began the most rewarding, impactful, and at times emotionally challenging month yet.

This topic felt completely different—and not only because there was only one recipient, with no postage required. While I had previously opted for simple, spare (affordable) cards, for Jake I splurged on a box of thick, cream-colored stationery and envelopes lined in a classic, colorful Florentine print. (We started officially dating my semester abroad in Florence, when Jake had come to visit and we kissed on the Ponte Vecchio.)

For the first time all year, I didn't write eight or ten cards in a two-hour burst. I wrote Jake one note every day. Generally, I would sit at my writing desk for a few focused minutes after putting the kids down, but sometimes I would write the card earlier, at my work space, and sometimes I would sneak it in while he was brushing his teeth, right before bed.

In preparation for the month, back in February I'd opened a note on my phone titled "Thank you, Jake" and had been adding to it all year. The list included "cleaning the blender before you left this morning," "singing 'To be loved!' every time the boys ignore you and call for me," and "being our family's master of logistics."

Those notes became the content for some of the cards. "Thank you for playing our wedding song in the morning, like you did back on February 1, and thank you for playing the chilled-out jazz mix from Charlie's birth this morning. Thank you for being the DJ of our house/lives. I love how you set a perfect mood with music." Another card read, "I had PMS one weekend in April, and wrote a note to myself that I felt 'overwhelmed and irritable, but Jake bought and made delicious steaks—so nice.' (Overwhelmed and irritable? I don't believe it!) Thank you for making me steak when I'm PMSing, and thank you for allowing my hormones and moods their due space."

But most often I wrote about whatever was currently happening. I thanked Jake for "getting the children back to sleep last night, and for staying up for those two hours listening, making sure they were getting back to sleep. Those boys are so lucky that you are theirs." And for "identifying potential danger at Nico's party this morning, and thank you for always thinking two steps ahead of our children's potential injuries. It must be exhausting in that head of yours. Thank you for being such a good daddy—the best. ('Men love when you call them Daddy.' —my mom.)"

I tried to make Jake laugh, even though, as Henry says, "It's Daddy's job to make jokes, and it's Mommy's job to laugh." One note was addressed directly to his muscles, which I thanked for working so hard to be "ripple-y." I thanked Jake for "being so legitimately excited for me to join you and your work friends at karaoke tonight. Thank you also for not acting embarrassed when I sang 'Shoop.'"

I thanked him for being a hero husband. For "making me delicious coffee and eggs this morning. Why do your coffee and eggs taste better than mine?" And for "taking a detour home to pick up the natural pink bubbly of my dreams." And for "all of your kitchen work today— unloading all dishes, taking out trash. The kitchen is a daily beast that needs feeding, and I'm so grateful you are on top of it and are my total partner, in that and all ways."

Oh, but this isn't fair, you might be thinking. *She married the perfect man!*

And I did. I really did. But know this: While rooting around my phone for that list of ways Jake impressed me throughout the year, I stumbled upon two other lists, from the previous fall. October's was titled "Stuff I take care of" and included, among many other chores: "constant neatening up and putting away," "remembering what we need (dish soap, diapers, wipes)," "managing kid clothing and shoes," "researching childcare," and "handling birthdays."

And I found this related list from last September, a series of conversation prompts: "I'd love if you could take off my plate . . . ," "I start to feel resentful when . . . ," "I could be wrong but it seems like there's tension when . . ."

I wasn't wrong; there had been tension that fall, a little over a year

Things I Thanked My Husband for in December

ago. Resentment had been building on both sides because we were each feeling as though we were doing more than the other person, and we hadn't yet figured out how to talk about it.

The truth was (and is) that with two busy careers and two little kids, we were *both* doing too much. On a podcast, I heard the organizational psychologist Adam Grant—the one who tweeted about thanking mentors—explain it this way: "You put a married couple in separate rooms, and you ask them for the total work that goes into their marriage—what percent are you responsible for? Three out of every four couples add up to over 100 percent. Somebody's lying. Men generally overestimated more than women did. But what's really interesting about this is, if you break down why, it's not because you want to think that you're inherently a better partner than your spouse. You want to believe that your spouse is the same kind of great partner that you are. It's more that *you were there for every act of generosity that you did.* You were present when you walked the kids to school. Whatever your partner's doing, you just can't recall that. So, I think it makes it hard to judge, because we know too much about ourselves, and we don't have a good comparison with other people."

The emphasis is mine because the words rang out like an alarm when I heard them. It's so simple it's almost dumb: We see everything we are doing because we are the ones doing it. And switching that mind-set—from being preoccupied with every little chore I handle, to noticing every task or favor Jake does—was enormously helpful in correcting the misconception that even equal partners have, that they alone are doing more than their fair share.

My friend Susan asked me whether the notes affected Jake's behavior. Did they give him an incentive to be extra helpful? It didn't seem so to me. But I asked Jake for his opinion. "Well, I didn't want the card at the end of the night to read 'Despite the following things, I guess . . .

thanks for whatever.' That's not what I was shooting for," he said. "But who's on their best behavior with two little kids? Maybe during the first two or three days I was conscious of it, a little bit. But after that I was just living my life. You can't be working for your card for an entire month."

How did it feel for Jake to be on the receiving end of all this gratitude? Here was how he explained it one morning late in the month as we walked to work together: "The notes had the opposite effect of the expression 'You're missing the forest for the trees,' which means, you know, 'You're focusing on the little things, and you're missing the big picture.' You and I say, 'I love you' a lot, and that is the forest, the love we have for each other. This month refocused us on the nice trees that make up the forest. Receiving all the notes made me feel appreciated for these little things that I do that make up the entirety of our relationship."

"Whereas sometimes," I clarified, "if we're not being mindful, it's easy to focus on the one or two diseased trees in the forest."

"Exactly that," he agreed. "It's more about problem solving. 'This tree has issues, let's talk about this, let's work through that.' The trees are, 'I love you *because this*. I love *that you do this*.' It was wonderful to feel seen for those trees—some big things and some small things as well. It was a wonderful way to end each evening. No matter what the day held, at the end of the night there was this card, and I'd feel appreciated and warm, and I went to bed happy."

Did he ever suffer from thank you note fatigue? In a word, no. "I don't think there's a day that goes by that I don't do something for you and you don't do something for me," Jake said. "Looking at all the cards, seeing it on paper, it made me think about all the little things that make our relationship work."

Gratitude Is Contagious

I don't want to exaggerate, but as I sit here at my desk—more than a year after writing Jake thirty-one thank you notes—I can say with confidence that the experiment changed the way we speak to each other. Last January, a few weeks after our gratitude month, Jake and I were riding in a rental car in Florida, and I recorded our conversation. I said that I'd noticed he'd been "extra sweet to me, and extra vocally appreciative. I felt like you had taken in what I was saying to you, and you were giving it back to me in a lot of different ways."

He replied, "When you feel seen, when you have that overwhelming feeling of being appreciated, you feel more open to telling the other person how you appreciate them."

"While I'm not writing you a thank you note every day anymore . . ."

"I've noticed," he deadpanned.

". . . I do feel like I have a slightly different approach. I feel like I am trying to acknowledge the stuff that you do, and I feel that you're doing the same for me, which makes things a little kinder and nicer."

"I think that's right," he said. "Thank you for writing me those notes. It meant a lot."

There's scientific evidence that expressing gratitude improves relationships. Sara Algoe, the director of the Emotions and Social Interactions in Relationships Laboratory at the University of North Carolina at Chapel Hill, posited what she called the "find-remind-and-bind theory of gratitude." Expressing gratitude to someone serves to find or remind you of the good in a relationship, and, she wrote, it "helps to *bind* recipient and benefactor closer together."

"Find-remind-and-bind" came from Algoe's 2008 study of a college sorority that followed members during a week of gift-giving. For a 2010 study of couples—called, relevantly, "It's the Little Things: Everyday Gratitude as a Booster Shot for Romantic Relationships"—

Algoe asked 134 people in heterosexual, cohabiting relationships to complete nightly diaries for two weeks, recording their own and their partner's thoughtful actions, their emotional response to interactions with their partner, and their relationship well-being. Every day, they assessed their own gratitude on a scale of one to five.

"Men and women with grateful partners," Algoe wrote, "felt more connected to the partner and more satisfied with the romantic relationship than they had the previous day." Gratitude, she concluded, "may work as a momentary reminder of the partner's good qualities, and help maintain or enhance the relationship." Furthermore, gratitude is, as Algoe wrote in her 2008 study, "probably best understood as a mechanism for forming and sustaining the most *important* relationships of our lives, those with the people we care about and count on from one day to the next."

I launched this project primarily to reconnect with the people and parts of myself that seemed to be slipping away. I was surprised to learn that gratitude also has the power to heal and improve one's closest relationships. The strongest tie I have is with Jake, and this month bound us closer together.

Giving Up Your Power Can Be the Ultimate Power Move

One note, from December 15, shows that thank you notes are not magic marriage bullets. "Thank you for talking it out," I wrote, "and making sure we figured it out as soon as possible. I love you, and I always will." My handwriting looks different—more spread apart, as if I knew I wouldn't have much to say but wanted to fill the card anyway. I remembered how difficult it was to write this card, because we'd had a terrible day. We'd argued, and I cried a lot, like, heave crying. Looking back, though, I couldn't recall what the fight was about.

The note from the day before offered a hint: "Thank you for drafting and sending those two emails to [Henry's teacher]. This is so difficult, and I'm grateful to have you as my partner, as together we will stop ourselves from murdering the kids who are hurting Henry."

I remembered Henry getting bullied in kindergarten, of course, but I still couldn't remember any of the particulars of this argument, and neither could Jake. Was our forgetfulness a way of glossing over something important? I searched the notes on my phone from that month and I found one titled, cryptically, "sight words." Reading the list, I remembered writing it between crying jags on my bed, prepping for the inevitable continuation of our argument while Jake was downstairs with the kids. "Sight words," it read. "Play dates. Doctor appointments. Christie—what did that mean?? Moving the car and getting the ticket. Hanukkah presents? I'm the one who's actually doing this shit and you are criticizing."

It was coming back to me, even if some of the details were lost. (I still don't know the answer to my question about Henry's speech therapist, "Christie—what did that mean??") I was feeling criticized and blamed—for not practicing Henry's "sight words," the words on flash cards that he was having trouble reading; for not making enough playdates for him, which might ease the social problems he was having at school; for parking the car in a spot that got us a ticket; for buying gifts for Christmas (my childhood holiday) but not Hanukkah (Jake's).

It was the same fight we'd been having since becoming parents: I am doing too much, and you're not doing enough. (Sometimes that complaint came from him, sometimes from me.) Only this fight escalated—why? A few reasons that I can see, in hindsight. We were both feeling an incredible amount of stress—from the upcoming holidays, yes, but mostly from learning that Henry was getting hurt. We felt frustrated and angry, and we weren't talking to each other about our feelings, so they were building.

On my side, feeling unappreciated stung more than usual. Handing over daily thank you notes for two weeks had felt like giving away my emotional armory piece by piece, and it had left me extra vulnerable.

I could feel in that moment, crying on my bed alone smack in the middle of my love month, the hazards of gratitude and why it's tempting to avoid it altogether. Throughout the year, I felt that reluctance. I felt it on a cellular level—a force trying to hold me back from freely expressing my gratitude.

That hesitation is thrown into sharpest relief with the person you feel most comfortable with, the person who does the most for you—your strongest tie. Not thanking that person to keep your own defenses intact is withholding something sacred. It's tit-for-tat thinking, and where does it get you? Obsessive lists on your phone that catalog all the laundry you're doing, all the possible conversation prompts for an argument that you want to win.

When Jake came upstairs that evening on December 15, I managed to stop crying and say my just-rehearsed piece. To my surprise, Jake started crying, too—and he, unlike me, is not a crier. He opened up about how helpless he felt about Henry being bullied (it's not about me), and he apologized for taking it out on me, and before long we were embracing.

Expressing gratitude did mean giving up some of my power. But in receiving that gratitude with an open heart and hearing me out, Jake had given up his power as well. We were both vulnerable, and that made us better at communicating.

That's the value in handing over your power. *Here, you have it. Take it all*, I was saying, not knowing whether it was brave or foolish to relax my grip. Give it a try. You might be surprised at how easily they give it back.

When Jake spotted the note on the nightstand before bed, he said that it must have been hard to write.

It was. But this month showed me that our marriage works best when we choose to communicate instead of close off, and when we choose kindness over self-pity.

Here was what writing Jake thirty-one thank you notes did: It showed both of us how good it felt to be acknowledged for everything we did, and that realization changed the way we talked to each other.

Here was what writing Jake thirty-one thank you notes did not do: Check off a thank you box. A thank you to a partner is not one and done. It is not thirty-one and done. Expressing gratitude has become part of the maintenance of our marriage.

On a Saturday the following May, I woke up and took an exercise class, showered, and headed into Manhattan to run *a thank you note writing seminar*. When I returned, Jake was making dinner after a rough day with the kids, and he pointed out that I really hadn't thanked him for handling everything that day. I jotted down in my notebook: "He doesn't need a card. He *does* need an acknowledgment.

I need to give that to him instead of thinking, oh, I did the same and more two weeks ago while you were prepping for your trial."

Then, in August, I spent an entire Sunday at a coffee shop working on *a book about thank you notes* and came home to find Jake feeling upset because I didn't thank him for the time he gave me.

Marriage takes work. It's a cliché, and my years of editing and writing have trained me to delete clichés. But like so many others—*The days are long, but the years are short*—this one is true, just not in the way I imagined. I used to think that only bad marriages took work. Jake and I spent years essentially cuddled up on our abnormally deep couch, feeling smug about our relationship. There was the occasional misunderstanding, and even full-on argument, but those we took pride in—because we handled them so quickly, completely, and compassionately. That work was almost cute.

But things have changed since having kids. Now prioritizing our relationship takes actual work, and this is the work: We swallow our own pride and sense of righteousness and express our gratitude. It's a daily task, and like the laundry, it piles up if we ignore it.

Jake and I still say "I love you" a lot. But just like Henry added the phrase "I'm grateful for you" into his repertoire, I now regularly say to Jake, "You take such good care of us." That's what the month helped me see, exactly how good he is at that.

Something else became clear, which I wrote to him on the penultimate day of December: "This thought has rung through my head during my year of gratitude: Lucky in love, lucky in love, lucky in love. That's me—thanks to you."

My final note was written on a thin sheet torn off a memo pad from Ann Arbor's Campus Inn. "I'm all out of those cards," I explained, "but this note is nice too, as it comes from our place of origin. OK, not Acapulco, where we met, or Italy, where we fell in love . . . but the place where we settled into a routine and figured out how to be a couple. Thank you for telling me you love me the day you picked me up from the airport our senior year. Thank you for all the nicknames you've given me since, and for always making me feel loved, special, content, safe. I love you, Jakie."

HOW TO WRITE NON-CHEESY LOVE LETTERS

1. *Open your eyes.* What is your partner doing for the house? For your well-being?

2. *Capture the details.* In love letters, as in all writing, specific is better than generic.

3. *Recall memories.* Maybe you're reminded of a special trip you took or something your partner once said.

4. *Share your feelings.* Whether you're writing about something that happened today or years ago, describe the way it made you feel.

5. *Notice and then reject this thought:* "Yeah, they did this one chore, but I did that and more last week."

6. *Be vocal about your own needs.* Once you're expressing gratitude more regularly, you'll likely start to feel more of it coming your way. If you aren't, ask for that recognition.

CHAPTER THIRTEEN

LOOKING BACK

How Writing Thank You Notes Can Lead to an Active Gratitude Habit

LESSON: This year was only the beginning.

BENEFIT: Expressing gratitude has made me a happier person.

SURPRISE: Gratitude is a pathway back.

still had thirty thank you notes to write. Why, oh, *whyyyyy* had I scrapped my home month in June?

I'd been brainstorming potential makeup topics. I thought of personal/beauty—"people who make me feel good"—but I got only as far as my hair stylist, Jeff. I briefly considered fitness, but that seemed to overlap with health. (And really, who did I think I was?) The near winner was kids: I would address all the notes to Henry and Charlie, just as I'd done for Jake. "Hook each note onto something they said, and thank them for that quality," I wrote. It's a sweet idea, and one I might execute in the future. But at that moment, creating thirty meaningful mementos for my children felt like . . . a lot. Already in December I had mailed out the thirty family postcards I wrote at the end of November and written Jake a note every night, all while working too many hours and hosting family and managing the

holidays. I needed to find a topic that was undemanding, with a template that could further ease the way.

Ever since I'd gone public with this project in October, so many people had showed their support—from family members to strangers on Instagram. I felt I had a cheering section, and there was an obvious way to thank them.

This Year Was Only the Beginning

I'd given myself permission to complete the final thirty notes in January. I'd blown past deadlines throughout the year, after all. What was the difference? Who would know, or care?

In the relative quiet of late December, after family members had departed and the wrapping paper was recycled, I wrote my list of Thank You Year cheerleaders while sitting on the couch with Jake, and I mentioned that I planned to finish the notes over the next few weeks.

"Really?" he asked. "Don't you want to finish this before the end of the year? I'll give you that time if you need it."

It was a glimpse of how supportive he would be throughout the process of writing this book, when he would whisk the kids away for the day or the weekend to let me write. And so, with Jake's help, I hunkered down in the final two days of the year. I wrote to extra-supportive friends who'd encouraged me to keep going. I thanked

Instagram followers who were documenting their own gratitude journeys. I thanked the social scientist Amit Kumar, the first gratitude expert I'd contacted. I thanked my favorite librarian, Beth, for "spreading the concept to students at your school."

I thanked stationers like Caroline, who'd sent me notes of encouragement and samples of their beautiful cards. "I absolutely love my Scribble & Daub hand-painted cards (so much that I am treasuring them, which is why I'm not writing on one now—I hope you don't mind!)" It was one of a few traditional thank you notes I wrote this month—the kind that I used to dismiss as mere transactions. But I'd come around on those. Thank you cards for gifts were more fun to write now, using all the tips I'd accumulated. I wrote a template for the beginning ("Thank you so much for your enthusiastic support of my Thank You Year!"). Then I went deeper than was required, offering that Caroline's was part of a "warm, positive reaction" that "has served as fuel to finishing it."

I wrote the last card to Henry. "All year long, while I've been writing one thank you card for every day of the year, you have been so supportive. You keep saying that what I'm doing is 'awesome,' and that has really helped me keep going—knowing that you are paying attention, and that you're proud of me. I've loved when you've helped me write the cards—to the people who gave money to City Harvest in January, and to the book authors in October. I'm proud of YOU—that you're learning how important it is to tell people thank you and let them know how you feel. I love you, honey."

On the afternoon of December 31, hours before we were about to host a New Year's Eve dinner for fourteen—Jake, I'm admitting publicly that you were right, and that was too much to take on—I finished. I had been so focused on completing the project that I hadn't

thought about how writing that final card would feel. I was sitting on a low stool, writing on my tiny vanity. I felt warmth spread to my fingers and toes. When I glanced up, I caught myself in the mirror with the biggest smile. I took a picture to remember the feeling.

As meta as this last exercise was—thanking the Thank You Year supporters—it was also meaningful. It allowed me to reflect on the project as a whole and meditate on its greater significance. I felt incredibly (there is no better word) *grateful* for my recaptured friendships, stronger relationships, and new connections. I felt grateful for the whole process. And I was determined to find a way to keep it up beyond this one year.

Expressing Gratitude Has Made Me a Happier Person

Initially I wondered whether the short-term joy of writing the notes would lead to a boost in my overall happiness. Now I knew the answer. My note writing had become so much more than a quick-fix mood lifter—although it was that, too. The 365 notes had a cumulative effect. Still today, I feel lighter. I have more patience with my kids (some days). In bed at night, before closing my eyes, I find myself smiling. Naming the people in my life, and thanking them, and cementing those relationships has made me happier.

"If you think it's happiness that makes you grateful, think again," Brother David Steindl-Rast said in his popular TED Talk. "It's gratefulness that makes you happy. . . . Grateful people are joyful people, and joyful people—the more and more joyful people there are, the more and more we'll have a joyful world."

I believe the year has raised my happiness "set-point," as positive psychologists call it. As Robert A. Emmons explains in his book *Thanks!: How Practicing Gratitude Can Make You Happier*: "Most people who diet are familiar with the notion of set-points. Despite their best efforts, weight loss is notoriously difficult to maintain as a metabolic pull of sorts encourages weight to return to previous levels. There is a similar set-point for happiness levels: researchers suggest each person has a chronic or characteristic level of happiness. According to this idea, people have happiness set-points to which they inevitably return following disruptive life events. Getting that book published, moving to California, having the person of your dreams answer your personal ad—each of these may send the happiness meter right off the scale for a while but, in a few months, it will drift back to the set-point that is typical for that individual."

The happiness set-point is genetically determined, Emmons explained. And I was blessed with a high one. I'm the person who, as a child, would sprint and jump into bed, excited to read about Ramona Quimby, or Matilda, or Heidi, or Jo March. I'm the person who sat with my boss Lisa one Monday morning, telling her that I had a great weekend despite the food poisoning. The intervening years had dampened that relentless cheeriness. The cards reminded me who I was, helping me reclaim that optimism.

It turns out that gratitude is one of the few known ways to increase your happiness set-point. Emmons ran a study for which some participants kept gratitude journals, and the gratitude group was, as he explained in *Thanks!*, "still enjoying benefits *six months later*. . . . They maintained levels of overall well-being that were nearly 25 percent higher than persons in the control condition. The evidence contradicts the widely held view that all people have a set-point of happiness that cannot be reset by any known means."

Emmons goes on to discuss Martin Seligman (known as the "founder of positive psychology") and his University of Pennsylvania study that instructed participants to write and deliver a letter of gratitude to someone who "had been especially kind to them or who made an enormous positive difference . . . who had never been properly thanked." One week after the exercise, participants experienced a significant boost in happiness and a drop in depressive symptoms, benefits that were maintained even a month later.

You probably get the point by now, but it bears repeating: Feeling gratitude is crucial, but expressing it is where the magic happens.

Gratitude Is a Pathway Back

Just as the notes helped me manage stress throughout the year, they now assuaged my holiday anxiety.

The December before I launched my Thank You Year, I walked

around my neighborhood feeling like Scrooge, grumbling about the fairy lights on the brownstones and Christmas trees that seemed like artifice in a cold, scary world. I was practically rolling my eyes at that young girl, me, who had once sung "Silent Night" to herself by the twinkling tree.

In the final month of my Thank You Year, I embraced the craziness of the holidays despite the continued craziness of the world. I took in the small moments—baking oatmeal-cherry cookies with Charlie and eating them with my dad; eavesdropping as Henry and Charlie cooked up a plan to catch Santa in the act; sitting down to eat lobster ravioli that Jake and his brother made as part of our Feast of the Seven Fishes. I had trained myself to look around, and I cherished what I saw. I kept thinking, *I am so glad to be here.*

I spent the last moments of the year surrounded by New Year's Eve dinner party guests. There was Alonso from Berlin, whom I'd written to in my travel month. There were Nick and Ro, in from Minneapolis, who'd received cards in my friends and mentors and food months. There was Mollie, who racked up notes as a mentor, neighbor, and Thank You Year cheerleader. There was Jake, of course. Charlie was in bed upstairs; Henry had fallen asleep on the couch. Throwing a fourteen-person dinner party was too much to take on, to be sure. But it allowed for the moment when I looked around and took it all in.

This December, twelve months after my Thank You Year ended, I treated myself to a Broadway matinee—it's my one-person company's annual holiday tradition. This would be the last show that I would see for a good long while, as three months later Covid-19 closed down the theaters. I chose *A Christmas Carol*. Campbell Scott played Scrooge, who, in the last act, as we all know, changes his perspective and rejoices in his life. "I feel as giddy as a schoolboy!" he says. Belle Fezziwig, his old love interest, tells him, "Change is within all of us. It's why life is such a thrill."

As Scrooge gets ready to celebrate, he invites the audience to join: We passed forward platters and sent oranges shooting down long strips of fabric from the mezzanine. Scrooge pulled up a man named Tom and led him backstage; Tom then came out holding a towering dessert. It was all so delightful that I found myself sobbing. When snow came falling down above us, the man in a buzz cut sitting next to me gasped audibly. In the last moments of the show, the actors played "Silent Night" on handbells. I felt like the girl I once was, in utter awe of the season and the lights and the goodness that lies in each of us.

Maybe this is my redemption story after all. My Thank You Year didn't carry me from stingy to generous, or from miserable to happy, or from cruel to kind. But it allowed me to look outside myself and my lists and really see other people. It helped me go from disconnected to connected, from distracted to present, from autopilot to pilot, from cranky and busy to joyful and optimistic. *Sometimes.* Most of the time.

Gratitude *is* optimism. It's choosing to see the contours of what's there instead of the shadows of what's missing. And gratitude is a pathway back—to a friendship, to hobbies you once loved, to identities you've shed. It's a pathway back to yourself. The word "gratitude" once grated on me—I avoided it when naming this project. Now I've fully embraced the word, as I have so much else that's vulnerable and embarrassing and uncool.

If this book has felt like a love letter to my husband, my family, my neighborhood, my friends, that's because it is. Thank you notes helped me fall in love with my too hectic, often messy, deeply imperfect, very lucky, absolutely miraculous life. And expressing gratitude can do the same for you, too.

HOW TO KEEP UP AN ACTIVE GRATITUDE PRACTICE

Here are some things I've been trying without the rigors of a Thank You Year.

1. *Make a dedicated thank you note folder.* I bought a leather folder that has compartments for cards, with a pen and stamps on one side and a notebook where I list people to thank on the other. I keep the folder handy for when I might have ten or fifteen minutes to write.

2. *Start Thankful Thursdays.* Inspired by Beth the librarian in Virginia, I try to write a few thank you notes on Thursdays around lunchtime.

3. *Write notes as a weekend project.* If you have kids, you know the weekend can stretch on. Decorating cards and writing thank you notes is a great project to do together, and it gives you an opportunity to teach kids how to live a grateful life.

4. *Express gratitude any way you like.* When you experience a fleeting moment of happiness, hold on to it, and tell the person or people responsible. That could be verbally, by text, or (and by now you know this one's my favorite) in a card.

ACKNOWLEDGMENTS

It's a lukewarm word, "acknowledgment." I'd like to not only acknowledge but wholeheartedly thank the following people (some for not the first time in this book).

♥ Alison Fargis, my agent and champion, for believing in this project from the start and for shepherding it so well.

♥ Marian Lizzi, as well as the entire TarcherPerigee team, for putting your trust in me and allowing me the freedom to write the book I wanted to write.

♥ Kelly Lasserre, for creating beautiful artwork and for patiently dealing with my vanity and reworking my portrait.

♥ Amit Kumar, for being my gratitude science guru and for responding so quickly to all my emails. And Gillian Sandstrom, Cory Allen, and Giacomo Bono, for giving thoughtful interviews, and Bret Stetka, for weighing in on the brain science.

♥ Susan Chumsky, for offering unobtrusive, superlative suggestions. The book is better because of you. And Pam Kaufman, for sending sharp notes and for the term "Mayberry, with mozzarella."

♥ Lu and Mom and Sara and Julie, for allowing me to get personal.

♥ Emma Straub, for helping me navigate the publishing world at every stage of this book's life.

♥ Jenny Rosenstrach, for taking my project public. And Joanna Goddard, for publishing Jenny's post and for writing a blurb for the proposal.

♥ Brigitte Hamadey and Mari Heller, for giving helpful feedback on my book proposal.

♥ Jake, for taking the kids to Lulu & Popeye's so I could write alone in the house, and for believing in me since reading my first column in *The Michigan Daily*, and for making me laugh within minutes of meeting and every day since.

♥ To a ten-year-old girl in her floral bedroom, surrounded by dog-eared books and wild dreams, for the stubborn optimism. We got here eventually, you and me.

♥ Finally, you, the reader. I felt you there with me while I was writing, and you were kind, compassionate, and forgiving of my flaws. You laughed at anything even approaching a joke. Thank you for spending this time with me. I hope you found inspiration to write to a long-lost friend, or your partner, or a neighbor. If you ever get stuck or feel squirmy, email me at gina@ginahamadey.com.

ABOUT THE AUTHOR

GINA HAMADEY is the former travel editor at *Food & Wine* and *Rachael Ray Every Day,* and she started her career at *O, The Oprah Magazine* and *George.* Her writing has appeared in those publications as well as in *Reader's Digest, Real Simple,* and *Women's Health.* She founded the content marketing agency Penknife Media, and wrote *¡Buenos Nachos!* She lives in Brooklyn with her family.

ginahamadey.com

@gina.hamadey

@gina_hamadey

THANK
YOU ♥